Simon Rose has written a bewilde  of them with Steve Caplin. A wi.. for Screenwriting, he wrote the movie *The Flying Scotsman*, starring Jonny Lee Miller and Brian Cox. The former film critic of the *Mirror*, he now reviews movies each week for the BBC's General News Service.

Steve Caplin is an award-winning photomontage artist whose work appears in newspapers and magazines including the *Guardian*, the *Sunday Telegraph* and *Radio Times*. Steve is the author of several books on computer graphics, writes a fortnightly column in *MacUser* magazine, and gives live and online lectures on Photoshop. He is the founder of the Photoshop artists' image library *thefullmontage.com*.

Complete and utter
ZEBU

Simon Rose
&
Steve Caplin

Old St PUBLISHING

First published in 2009 by Old Street Publishing Ltd
40 Bowling Green Lane, London EC1R 0NE
www.oldstreetpublishing.co.uk

ISBN 978-1-906964-33-7

10 9 8 7 6 5 4 3 2 1

A CIP catalogue record for this title is available from the British
Library.

Typeset by Steve Caplin.
Printed and bound in Great Britain by Cox & Wyman Ltd.

Introduction

DECEIT IS DESTROYING our society.

Fibs, spin, bullshit, propaganda, whoppers, porkies. Call them what you will, lies are everywhere. Integrity is out fashion, replaced by the attitude that if we fall for the bullshit, then it's our fault for being so gullible. The public is there to be fleeced, not served.

We're used to politicians bamboozling us with statistics and lying with impunity, knowing we won't remember what they said a few months later. They lay down the law for the rest of us, pontificating about benefit cheats, while bleeding the public purse for their tax-free expenses. Then, when they're caught, they bleat pathetically that it was 'within the rules' – omitting to mention that they drew up the rules in the first place.

It isn't just politicians who are lying to us. Whichever way we turn, we are surrounded by lies. Advertising is supposed to be 'legal, decent, honest and truthful', but too often its real aim is to mislead us while staying just within the law.

Day after day, we're lied to by estate agents, insurance companies, manufacturers, civil servants, health advisers, retailers, photographers, airlines, restaurants and television programmes. And how can we believe what *anyone* says when even our language is losing its meaning?

Although the big lies make the headlines, it's the small, everyday, throwaway half-truths that, bit by bit, are wearing away our ability to trust. We have to weed out truth from fiction in even the tiniest of transactions, and it's leaving us confused, angry and worn out.

This book is a miscellany of the misinformation that mars modern life. Its aim is to open our eyes to the hypocrisy, dishonesty and prevarication assailing us on all sides.

Authors Steve and Simon hold opposing political views. The liberal Steve points out that the book may seem anti-Labour, but it's really just anti-government; it's Labour's bad luck that it's been in power since 1997. Libertarian Simon thinks that's *our* bad luck. We like to think our individual biases have cancelled each other out, making for an even, balanced rant.

In researching the book, we've been incensed by the way so many organisations and officials think nothing of deliberately, calculatingly and cold-bloodedly misleading us. They've broken an unwritten contract of trust, but when they're found out we're lucky if we even get an apology. The diet of daily deception is corroding the very fabric of society. The MPs' expenses scandal woke us all up to our legislators' outrageous behaviour. But the rot goes so much deeper. We hope this book will help cure us of our collective blindness.

It's time to fight back against the lies we're bombarded by every day. We deserve to be told the truth. We are not stupid. We know we're not. After all, don't Government ministers keep quoting exam statistics that prove we're getting cleverer all the time?

This book could have been much bigger, but while we'd love you to throw the book at the lying bastards we don't want to be held responsible for you killing them. If you want to get involved, visit *utterzebu.com* and share your own stories of complete and utter zebu.

As Peter Finch's character in the movie *Network* famously yelled out: 'I'm mad as hell and I'm not going to take this any more.' We're mad as hell, and you should be too.

Steve Caplin & Simon Rose
London, October 2009

'A lie gets halfway around the world before the truth
has a chance to get its pants on.'
Winston Churchill

'The size of the lie is a definite factor in causing it to
be believed, because the vast masses of a nation are
in the depths of their hearts more easily deceived
than they are consciously and intentionally bad.
The primitive simplicity of their minds renders them
more easy victims of a big lie than a small one.'
Adolf Hitler

British steak: it isn't British, and it isn't steak

NOT ONLY MIGHT the 'British' steak you order in a pub or restaurant not be British, it might not even be steak – or at least not as most of us think of it. In 2007, ITV's 'Undercover Mum' spirited some meat away from Wetherspoon pubs and sent it off for DNA analysis. Four out of six steaks were not British meat as claimed; they weren't even from cows. They were, in large part, from something called a zebu. The programme also found that three out of nine Hungry Horse pubs sold zebu meat as beef.

Zebu? Originating in India, these unattractive, jowled, hump-backed animals are now bred for meat in Africa, Asia and

arid parts of South America. Most of our zebu meat comes from Brazil, where zebus were imported early in the 20th century and crossed with Charolais cattle to become azebuados.

Although it's obviously in their interest to say so, the British-based National Beef Association considers zebu tougher and inferior to British beef. However, despite the distance travelled,

Brazilian zebu beef is cheaper. This is partly because, although beef production within the EU is stringently regulated, things are laxer in Brazil, the world's biggest beef exporter. The use of growth hormones is widespread and, in 2005, there was a foot and mouth outbreak in three provinces.

Although the EU then forbade imports from the provinces, supplying almost two-thirds of its beef imports, Brazilian imports barely dropped. The mystery was solved when John Bryan of the Irish Farmers' Association saw cattle being moved freely from those provinces into disease-free areas and exported from there.

Anyone who cares about the Amazonian rainforest might want to steer clear of Brazilian meat, as the cattle industry is a major cause of deforestation. In addition, two-thirds of slave workers freed by Brazil's Anti-Slavery Enforcement Team come from cattle ranches.

In 2008, the EU banned Brazilian beef imports for a time and now permits them only from approved farms. In 2009, the EU's own Food & Veterinary Office found half the farms they inspected didn't meet required standards, but the European Commission considers their findings 'minor deficiencies'. In the meantime zebu imports from countries like Namibia have climbed steeply.

Back in 2007, a Hungry Horse spokesman claimed that zebu beef was just as good as cattle farmed in the UK and was very good value; they wouldn't tell us whether they were still selling zebu in 2009. A Wetherspoon spokesman insisted they no longer sell zebu, yet their menu states that their steaks are sourced from, among other places, South America and Namibia – where only zebu breeds can survive.

These are not isolated incidents. In 2008, the BBC carried out an investigation among pubs and restaurants in the south-west of England. Eight of the forty samples they tested claimed to be 'British' or 'local' beef, but were actually zebu.

If you find your steak is tougher than usual, perhaps it's not cow but zebu. Where's your DNA testing kit when you need it?

On the plus side, Zebu is a very useful Scrabble word.

I promise to pay the bearer on demand

LOOK AT ANY £20 note, and you'll see the words 'I promise to pay the bearer on demand the sum of twenty pounds' beside the signature of the Chief Cashier of the Bank of England. But what does this promise actually mean?

It used to be that banknotes were simply promissory notes – IOUs, if you will – that really could be exchanged for gold coins. By 1925, the Bank would only give out gold in multiples of 400 ounces, so you couldn't just walk in with a fiver and walk out with a bag of tiny ingots.

When Britain finally abandoned the gold standard in 1931, the banknote became 'fiducary': that is, 'involving trust'. Which means that in order for banknotes to have any value whatsoever, all we have to do is, er, trust the bankers.

So do the words now have any meaning at all? Only in a very watered-down form. The phrase guarantees that the Bank of England will take any banknote we present to them, even if it's old or damaged, and give us the face value in the form of a spanking new banknote. If you were to take in a £1 note from 1797, for example, they'd hand over a shiny £1 coin for it. But frankly you'd be better off taking it to numismatists Spink, who in 1993 sold one for £57,200.

What the phrase really means, of course, is that you have a pocketful of broken promises.

Hollywood boob jobs: the virtual solution

WE'RE ALL USED to tales of Hollywood actresses having breast augmentation – in fact it's unusual to find an actress who *hasn't* had some kind of surgical enhancement.

Keira Knightley, however, is famously proud of her elfin figure. So she was not best pleased when the poster for her film King Arthur made more of her assets than nature had intended, thanks to the power of Photoshop.

Perhaps Ms Knightley's concerns over image manipulation trouble her less when she's pocketing a huge fee. As the face of Coco Chanel, she is once again the subject of considerable

● *Left: Spot the difference – Keira Knightley in the King Arthur poster, before and after. Above: the boob enhancers have been at it again.*

enhancement – although it has clearly been accomplished in the best possible taste.

It's a different matter, though, when the actress concerned is a child. When the posters for *Harry Potter and the Order of the Phoenix* were redesigned for the IMAX version, some marketing executive clearly decided that Emma Watson's charms weren't prominent enough for the true big screen experience – and they were duly enhanced. 'The mistake was promptly rectified and the poster taken down,' admitted a shame-faced Warner Brothers spokesman after the ensuing uproar.

● *How young is too young? Emma Watson was 17 when a Warner Brothers exec decided to increase her sex appeal.*

ice cream

Ice cream is made from cream, right? Wrong. Unless it's specifically labelled as 'dairy ice cream', it doesn't even have to have any milk content whatsoever – let alone any cream. Most ice cream is in fact made from hydrogenated palm kernel oil. Vanilla flavour ice cream doesn't even need to contain any real vanilla.

According to the Food Labelling Regulations 1996, for an ice cream to proudly bear the 'dairy' label it must contain – wait for it – at least 2.5% milk 'protein'.

Two and a half percent! And that's just the good stuff! What on earth are we feeding our children?

flavour

Banana flavour, chocolate flavour, roast moose flavour. They may sound tempting, and full of natural goodness, but they're almost certainly just chemically produced tastes with no banana, chocolate or moose in them at all.

Only if there is 'd' on the end will you get the real thing: 'chocolate flavoured' means the item has actually been flavoured with chocolate; 'chocolate flavour' simply means it tastes more or less like chocolate. And that's surely a matter of opinion.

—————— I wish I hadn't said that ——————

'I was not lying. I said things that later on seemed to be untrue.'

Richard Nixon, 1978, who resigned from office after being implicated in the Watergate scandal.

● *0 to 60 in... hang on, there's no 0. This speedometer starts at 5!*

Your sneaky speedometer

WE RELY ON the speedometers in our cars to give us an accurate, reliable indication of the speed at which we're driving. But, as an increasing number of drivers have found since fitting Sat Nav systems, the speed shown is often around five miles an hour higher than your true velocity. If you're driving through a 50 mph speed camera-monitored stretch of motorway and someone breezes past you at 55mph, the chances are you'll see a Sat Nav fixed to their windscreen.

It's called 'optimism' in the trade, and it's intended to safeguard the maker against manufacturing margins of error. Some more cynical conspiracy theorists, of course, believe it's all a government plot to force motorists to drive slower.

A glance at the speedometer design should prove the point: almost all of them show equal gradations between 10 and 20 mph, between 20 and 30, and so on, but there's usually only half that distance between 10mph and 0.

It's painful to admit, but even your car is lying to you.

homemade

In an era of homogeneity, what could be more welcoming than popping into a lovely pub with, chalked up on the blackboard, 'homemade soup' and other delicious-sounding nosh? Sadly, when trading standards officers in North Wales toured pubs, restaurants and hotels in March 2009 they found that on average, over a fifth of all food descriptions were misleading. While independent companies were responsible for only 16% of the errors, the national chains told whoppers so enormous that 47% of their descriptions were wrong.

Among the mistakes, they discovered 'homemade' soup bought in – and frozen; 'Welsh lamb casserole' that was actually a supermarket ready meal containing non-Welsh lamb; 'Cardigan Bay mackerel' and 'local sea bass' made from imported fish; and 'locally-farmed' turkey that would have had to travel for weeks if it had chosen to walk. Again and again, they found that terms such as 'Welsh', 'fresh', 'homemade', 'traditional' and 'local' were bandied about with no regard for the truth.

Readers of the BBC's news website were invited to send in their own examples, the best of which came from a man who had tried, in vain, to explain to a member of staff in a cafe that 'fresh cream' was not the stuff you squirt out of a can.

Richard Powell, chair of the North Wales Quality and Metrology Panel, said: 'The survey will be repeated later this year and authorities may take legal action against businesses found to be misleading consumers.' *May* take legal action? Wow, they must be quivering in their boots.

● *The group photograph – and, right, the man who didn't turn up.*

The Minister for fakes

SIX LOCAL MPs posing for a photo op at Tameside General Hospital. Unfortunately, James Purnell, the Secretary of State for Media, Culture and Sport, arrived late. So he posed in the same location and was rather clumsily digitally dropped into the group shot.

Purnell denied knowing anything about it. 'I didn't think a faked photo would be produced and I didn't see this photo before it went out, and if I had done wouldn't have agreed to it'.

Unfortunately, an email from the hospital's chief executive to him said otherwise. 'Dear James, Thank you for attending on Friday. I am pleased we were able to catch the photographer so that he could "drop you into the photographs".'

It might have been less embarrassing had the Culture Secretary not, just a fortnight earlier, attacked broadcasters over fixed phone-ins: 'In both politics and television you devalue the only currency you have if you forfeit the trust of the public.'

'Fish with your wine, sir – or in it?'

LOOK AT THE LABEL on almost any bottle of wine and it will say: 'Contains sulfites'. It won't actually mention grapes but chances are they're in there too. Sulfites shouldn't be anything to worry about. After all, 5-40 milligrams of sulfites per litre are produced naturally during the wine-making process as the yeasts convert sugar into alcohol. Wine-makers may add more to stop the wine going off, even though some people claim that sulfites hinder the body's ability to process alcohol properly and so worsen hangovers.

But, unless organic, there's a lot more to wine than just grapes and sulfites. Unfortunately for curious consumers, the EU has exempted alcohol producers from the usual food and drink labelling rules. They are permitted to use over 50 additives and preservatives in wine without telling us.

Wine-makers' aim in using additives is to make every bottle of their wine taste the same. According to Malcolm Gluck, the wine critic who wrote *The Great Wine Swindle*, 'Many, many wines are no better than a sort of alcoholic cola. You get artificial yeasts, enzymes, sugar, extracts, tannins, all sorts of things added.' Yet, he points out, 'The wine industry insists on this romantic notion that wine is just crushed grapes.'

There are many other appetising ingredients that might be used, such as charcoal, fish bladder extract (isinglass), copper sulphate, dried ox blood, caramel, hydrochloric acid, eggs, milk protein (casein), gelatin and – tripping easily off the tongue –

Ingredients that can legally be added to wine without notice

acacia (gum arabic)
allyl isothiocyanate
ammonium bisulphite
ammonium sulphate
argon
ascorbic acid
bentonite
betaglucanase
calcium alginate, carbonate, phytate, sulphate, tartrate, dioxide
casein
charcoal
citric acid
copper sulphate
diammonium phosphate
dimethyldicarbonate
gelatin
ion exchange resins
isinglass
kaolin
lactalbumin
lactic bacteria
lees
lysozyme
nitrogen
oak wood
ovalbumin (egg white)
oxygen
pectinolytic enzymes
plant proteins
polyvinylpolypyrrolidone
potassium alginate, bicarbonate, bisulphite, caseinate, ferrocyanide, metabisulphite, tartrate
silicon dioxide or colloidal solution
sorbic acid or potassium sorbate
sucrose
sulphur dioxide
tannin
tartaric acid
thiamine hydrochloride
urease
yeast cell walls
yeast mannoproteins

polyvinylpolypyrrolidone. Jacob's Creek Chardonnay, for instance, contains asorbic acid and tartaric acid, enzymes, milk powder and clay to help 'fine' the wine – making it less cloudy. Hardy's Merlot is finished off with gelatin, milk and eggs. Many cheaper wines have oak chips thrown in to give that desired 'aged in an old barrel' scent. Some wine-makers even add bentonite, an absorbent material which removes excess protein from white wine. Its other main use is in cat litter!

The days when Austrian producers were caught adding anti-freeze to sweeten their wines, as they did in 1985, are probably behind us. The same with the Italians who added methanol in 1987 and killed 23 people, although as recently as 2008 70 million litres of cheap wine were seized by the authorities and found to contain only 20% wine, the rest being made up of water, sugar, fertiliser, manure and even hydrochloric acid.

The only retailer in the UK that tells people what has gone to make the wine is The Co-op. Its Cape Pinotage label, for instance, lists the ingredients as: 'Grapes (Pinotage), Preservatives (Sulphur Dioxide), Tartaric acid. Made using: Yeast, yeast Nutrient (Diammonium phosphate). Cleared using: Bentonite, Pectinolytic Enzymes. Closure: Cork.'

In doing so, The Co-op is breaking the law and actually risks being prosecuted. As the chain admits, it 'is technically illegal, but in the consumer's interest'.

for illustrative purposes only

A curious phrase that has achieved currency on technology websites, next to the photograph of the item you're planning to buy. At first sight, it seems tautologous: what on earth could an image be for, if not for illustrative purposes?

The reality is a logical about-turn that's mind-boggling in its complacency. What the notice really means is that the photograph may not, in fact, be a true representation of the item you're trying to buy. The advertiser has the right to send you a different model or design after you've paid for it.

In other words, the only thing that can truthfully be said about the image is that it is probably *not* illustrative of the actual product.

'*If nominated I'll decline. If drafted I'll defer. And if elected I'll resign.*' Alex Salmond, denying his intention to stand as SNP leader, in June 2004

'*Let me be clear, from today I am not just launching a campaign to be SNP leader. Today I am launching my candidacy to be the first minister of Scotland.*' Alex Salmond, born-again SNP leadership candidate, in July 2004

Russian photo cheats are at it again

WE'RE ALL FAMILIAR with the Russian revolutionary photographs in which loyal party members who later turned out to be enemies of the state are airbrushed out of events. It's all part of the Stalinist paranoid need to rewrite history.

But that's all in the past, right? Not so. When Mikhail G. Delyagin, an outspoken critic of Vladimir Putin, took part in a televised debate it was decided that, as an official non-person, he should never have been there. And so, in retrospect, he wasn't: he was digitally removed from the broadcast.

Unfortunately, the job was botched. Although he certainly can't be recognised, there are certain shots in which the lower half of his body remains. His legs and hand are clearly visible to the right of the man holding the microphone, although his upper torso has been taken out. Well, if that doesn't shut him up, nothing will.

● *Removed from the broadcast: but is that the bottom half of a dissident sitting in the empty chair?*

up to

When the ill-fated Woolworths was facing its final hours, posters advertising 'Up to 50% off' were plastered over its stores' windows. Already beleaguered staff, facing the prospect of imminent unemployment, were treated to verbal attacks by bargain-hunting customers, furious at having been lured into a store in which only a tiny proportion of the goods on offer were sold at 50% off.

It's all down to the weasel words 'up to', of course. The phrase may be technically correct, but 'up to 50%' can mean anything from 1% upwards. It's an attention-grabbing device that has been used by commercial outlets for decades. The technique was fully employed by the now-defunct Allied Carpets, who regularly made offers such as 'Up to 50% off, plus an extra 20% off' – a meaningless concept, even when accompanied by the ubiquitous asterisks that provided the company with its standard get-out clauses.

The fat debate: fiddling the figures

SATURATED FATS are bad for your heart, right? Aren't they?

The report always quoted to support this claim dates back over 50 years to 1953, when Dr Ancel Keys, a psychologist, published 'Athersclerosis, a Problem in Newer Public Health'. He compared fat intake and death from heart disease in six countries and pointed out that the Americans, who ate most fat, had the most heart-related deaths while the Japanese, who consumed the least, had the fewest deaths.

The media, ever keen to take press releases at face value, accepted the findings hook, line and sinker. Governments around the world have, ever since, been lecturing us to cut down on saturated fats. In vain have other scientists pointed out that what the Keys study actually showed was a correlation between two things, not a causal link. The higher incidence of heart disease could, in fact, be caused by something else the Americans consumed more of than the Japanese: white bread, sugar, popcorn or even television.

Even more significantly, Keys chose six countries where the data most neatly supported his conclusions, and ignored 16 others that did not. Finland's mortality rate from heart disease, for instance, was 24 times that of Mexico. Their per-capita fat consumption? Practically identical. If he had used the data for all 22 countries, the link would have vanished.

More recent studies into fat consumption have tended not to demonise animal fats, particularly if they are part of a healthy diet with little processed food and a fair amount of exercise. So, next time an 'independent' body tells us we shouldn't do something, perhaps we should take it with a pinch of salt. Except salt's bad for us too.

simulated picture

On all advertisements for televisions, video and DVD players, a bright, colourful image will be displayed on the screen. It may be a still from a recent movie, a glossy photograph of a beach scene, or a beaming family snapshot. Whatever the image is, you can be sure it will be far higher quality than the actual picture displayed on the device you're being sold.

Why? Because if the studio lighting is sufficient for the photographer to capture the electronic equipment, it will be so bright that the screen looks dull and insipid in comparison. It's a reasonable point, which is why the images are always pasted on afterwards – but it doesn't detract from the fact that what we're being shown is not what we're actually purchasing. And when we buy a television, the quality of the picture on the screen *is* what we're buying; all the rest is mere packaging.

A simulated picture is little more than a serving suggestion, and a very poor one at that.

—— I wish I hadn't said that ——

'We found the weapons of mass destruction. We found biological laboratories ... And we'll find more weapons as time goes on. But for those who say we haven't found the banned manufacturing devices or banned weapons, they're wrong, we found them.'

George W Bush, 2003. No weapons of mass destruction were ever found in Iraq.

'It's all for a good cause': the great lottery rip-off

THE ODDS OF WINNING the UK's National Lottery jackpot are one in 13,983,816, less than the chance of being struck by lightning. But at least you have the satisfaction of knowing that your bet is doing some good. After all, as the National Lottery website says, 'Every single pound spent on the Lottery helps UK Good Causes.'

What? 'Every single pound?' Of all the porkies on all the websites in all the world, this is one of the biggest. It's a lie so enormous, you can see it from space. For a start, what about the prize money, without which nobody would ever buy a lottery ticket again? That accounts for 50% of total National Lottery revenue. Perhaps it was just a slip and they meant that all of the *rest* of the money spent on the lottery goes to good causes.

Not quite. First in the queue is the Government, which swipes 12% of the total in Lottery Duty. And then there's the sales commission of 5% to the retailers who sell the tickets. Another 5% goes to Camelot in operating costs and profits.

What actually does go to Good Causes should therefore be 28% of all the money wagered on the lottery. But out of that come the costs of the Lottery Commission, the quango overseeing the lottery. It doesn't come cheap and it's getting pricier. In 1999-2000 it paid out £1.37m in salaries. By 2007-8, that had gone up 93% to £2.65m, with another £72,000 distributed in bonuses. The Commission has also seen fit to spend £23 million on consultants.

Then there are the 15 bodies who decide which Good Causes should get money. They, too, have become costlier, their overheads rising from £145 million in 2003 to £205 million in 2008. The Big Lottery Fund, which hands out almost half of all money for Good Causes, has 1,000 staff and spends £77 million a year, 13% of its entire budget, on administration. When MPs

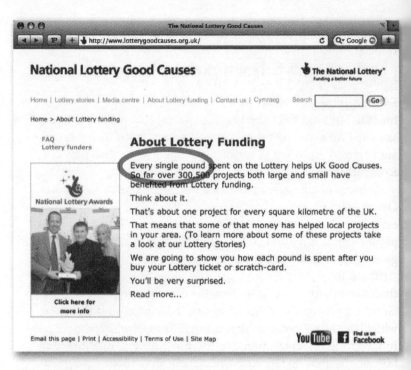

● *'Every single pound' is spent on Good Causes . . . so what about
the prize money?*

accused the regulators of being bloated, a spokeswoman for the
Department for Culture, Media and Sport said: 'It is perfectly
legitimate for a large-scale organisation like the National Lottery
to spend a small proportion of its income on administration and
core function costs.'

So which Good Causes actually benefit from the remaining
cash? The lottery was one of the few things anyone gives John
Major's Government credit for. 'My original vision for the
lottery,' said Major, 'was to fund a renaissance in sport, the arts
and our heritage.' Apparently this also included the Millennium
Dome, because every capital city just has to have a big tent.
When Labour came to power in 1997, Tony Blair was unusually
in agreement with Major: 'We don't believe it would be right to

use lottery money to pay for things which are the Government's responsibilties.'

In fact, the money spent on those Good Causes more than halved over the following decade. Sports grants dropped from £471 million in 1997-8 to £219 million in 2007-8, heritage funding fell from £474 million to £219 million and arts projects saw their money drop from £458 million to £219 million (figures are adjusted for inflation to 2008 prices). That's a 53% fall, with £746 million a year taken away.

Where has the rest of the money gone? With the London Olympics budget quadrupling from the original £2.4 billion estimate, £2.2 billion is being diverted from the Lottery to help pay for the games. £1 in every £5 allocated for Good Causes now goes towards paying for the Olympics.

In addition, Shadow Culture Secretary Jeremy Hunt claims that a whopping £4 billion has been diverted from the original Good Causes to the fields of health, education and transport which are the government's responsibilities and which should be funded from direct taxation. Money is being spend on things like libraries, school meals, hospice care and diagnostic equipment for hospitals. Good Causes, no doubt, but not quite what the Lottery was supposed to be for.

culling

Rats, termites and mosquitoes are 'killed'. Baby seals, deer and elephants are 'culled'. It sounds so much kinder.

The word originated in the 13th century, meaning merely 'to select from a group' – so we might produce an anthology by culling the best work from a selection of poets. Recently, it has come almost exlusively to refer to the practice of humanely disposing of unwanted members of a herd, flock or other group of animals.

They're still being killed, though.

pan-fried

Describing a Dover sole as 'fried' carries overtones of saturated fats, and makes it seem an unhealthy option. But when restaurants call an item 'pan-fried' it's an altogether more exotic description. But hang on a minute: how else can a Dover sole be fried? It's on a par with 'oven-roasted', a similarly redundant phrase. How long before we see potatoes described as 'saucepan-boiled'? Or salads as 'knife-cut'?

——— I wish I hadn't said that ———

'Mine is the first generation able to contemplate the possibility that we may live our entire lives without going to war or sending our children to war.'

Tony Blair, May 1997

● *US and Polish versions of the same Microsoft web ad: spot the difference.*

Empower your people – at least, some of them

WHEN MICROSOFT PRODUCED this online ad for their IT tools, they went out of their way to be politicall correct: a woman, an oriental man, and a black man. How very right on.

And how very right *off* of Microsoft's business unit in Poland, who decided to edit out the black man in favour of a more typically ethnic Pole.

Microsoft headquarters have issued a fulsome apology, of course – but will they continue to employ a Photoshop artist who's happy to show a white businessman with a black hand?

Insects, animal hair, rat shit: all the crap you can eat

'**THE CENTRAL GOAL** of the European Commission's food safety policy is to ensure a high level of protection of human health.' So says the Commission's Food Safety site. Quite right too.

Knowing this, we can laugh at America's lax regulations which permit so much of what the FDA calls 'filth' in their food that Ohio University researchers say each American eats about 'a pound or two of insects every year. One cannot see them, since they have been ground up into tiny pieces in such items as strawberry jams, peanut butter, spaghetti sauce, applesauce, frozen chopped broccoli, etc.'

Study of acceptable FDA guidelines make for enlightening, if queasy, reading. They allow up to:

- one maggot or five fly eggs in each 250ml of orange juice
- 50 insect fragments per 100g of peanut butter
- 9 mg of rodent excreta per kilogram of wheat
- 225 insect fragments or 4.5 rodent hairs per 225g of macaroni
- one pellet of rodent excreta in each sample of popcorn.

Each 100g of tomato juice can contain two drosophila maggots, or five eggs and one maggot, or ten eggs with no maggots.

Although the FDA terms these things 'repulsive', nutritionist Robert Choate claimed that there was more protein in the insects in American breakfast cereal than in the cereals themselves.

In Europe, the basic principles of legislation on contaminants in food are that: 'food containing a contaminant to an amount unacceptable from the public health viewpoint . . . shall not be placed on the market. Contaminant levels shall be kept as low as can reasonably be achieved following recommended good working practices.' So foodborne bacteria, toxins, lead, mercury and PCBs are heavily governed, as is genetic modification.

EU regulations define a contaminant as being 'any substance not intentionally added to food which is present in such food as a result of environmental contamination ... or as a result of the production, manufacture, processing, preparation, treatment, packing, packaging, transport or holding of such food.' But the regulations go on to say: 'the term "contaminant" does not cover insect fragments, animal hair and other extraneous matter.'

That's right. The EU does not care how much of what the FDA regard as 'filth' is in our food chain. It doesn't consider insects, animal hair and droppings to be food, so they are not covered by the regulations at all.

An article in the journal of the American Agricultural Law Association believes this is because 'EU policy places a higher priority upon free trade in food among member states than it does upon consumer health.' It points out that, under EU law, member states cannot prohibit, restrict or impede foods on the grounds that they contain bits of insect, animal hair or other extraneous matter. Nor are they allowed to use the 'precautionary principle', which is essentially taking the line 'better safe than sorry.' During a one-year period the FDA imposed 'import detentions' for 'filth' over 3,500 times, accounting for 31.5% of all detentions, though they don't say how many came from the EU. Suddenly, those American regulations don't seem so amusing.

Trying to look on the bright side, there is an argument that permitting such 'natural' contaminants in our food means fewer pesticides are used. And all those insects are full of protein, after all. Just not so sure about the rat faeces.

The camera lies: a political history

WE TEND TO ASSOCIATE the rise of falsified images with the appearance of Photoshop, and it's certainly true that the program has been responsible for many altered pictures. But long before computers or even cameras were invented, artists have been faking the truth for a variety of reasons.

Henry's dilemma

When Henry VIII was considering marriage to Anne of Cleves, he sent court portrait artist Hans Holbein to paint her likeness. In the days before EasyJet, there was no way Henry could get a look at her before she arrived for their wedding, by which time it would be too late to send her back.

Holbein, of course, had first to please the subject of his painting. And so he produced a rather flattering portrait of Anne, showing her as a demure if somewhat pale lady. Henry approved, and consented to her. With disastrous consequences: when she arrived, he was horrified. Holbein had far overstepped the mark, as the only other known portrait of Anne shows – and the marriage was never consummated.

● *Anne of Cleves, by Holbein (left) and Bruyn (right).*

● *Two striking battlefield shots by Alexander Gardner. The uniforms may vary, but the bodies are the same.*

The Civil War photographer

Even without resorting to studio trickery, photographers have long played fast and loose with the truth. Consider the example of the noted photographer Alexander Gardner, whose striking images of dead soldiers from both sides in the American Civil War brought him fame and fortune.

Except Gardner wasn't content merely to photograph the carnage he found. It turns out he used to drive a cartload of dead bodies from one picturesque battlefield location to another, dressing them up in appropriate uniforms and arranging them artfully in the scene. Compared with this, faking a photograph in Photoshop is tame.

The Soviet legacy

Nikolai Yezhov was the People's Commisar for Internal Affairs in the NKVD under Stalin. Nicknamed 'the Bloody Dwarf', he was at the height of favour in 1937. By 1938 he had fallen from grace – and so Stalin had him removed from official images, such as the one shown here. This early example of photomontage for political ends is an often-shown image, displaying the kind of underhand tricks those untrustworthy Commies used to get up to in their spare time.

But not all such photomontage was done for malicious purposes. The photograph opposite shows Lenin and his wife relaxing in their garden. A pleasant natural scene, with the

Russian leader shown in one of his more relaxed moments.

A pity, then, that the rifle of a guard standing nearby looked as though it was pointing right at the head of Lenin's wife. When later published, the guard and his weapon were removed. Faking the truth? Or is it merely acceptable cosmetic adjustment?

● *Nikolai Yezkhov before and after being airbrushed from history*

● *The Lenins at rest. Shame about the rifle barrel . . .*

The Kerry issue

Fast forward half a century to the 2004 US Presidential Election, in which John Kerry was standing as a Democrat against George W. Bush. His opponents claimed that he was an anti-war peace campaigner during the Vietnam conflict, and they produced photographs of him appearing with noted pacifist Jane Fonda at a peace rally.

● *Kerry and Fonda: original images below.*

Except he never attended the rally. The image was a simple montage that nonetheless achieved its purpose. Enough people were taken in by the deception, and Kerry lost the election.

Speed humps: the sleeping killers

WHOEVER CAME UP with the gruesome euphemism 'traffic calming' deserves their own special section of Hell, one where ex-motorists can take time out to exact revenge for years of motoring misery, preferably by driving over the gormless nerk at a painfully low speed. Pegged out beside him should be the borough engineer who first decided that the best way to get traffic to go more slowly was to stick a lump of raised tarmac across the road.

We all know the reality of 'sleeping policemen'. Vehicles brake before the bump then speed up to the next causing extra noise and vibrations, while low-slung cars can actually scrape their chassis. They are a menace for bus passengers. Bus company Trent Barton complains on its website that road bumps reduce service reliability, cause discomfort and put passengers at physical risk if there's a bump near a bus stop. They also cause damage to modern low-floor buses, leading to higher fares. 'At a time when central government, local authorities and bus operators are doing all they can to encourage greater use of buses, traffic calming schemes which result in greater discomfort, added danger, less convenience and extra expense for bus users, are unwelcome to say the very least.'

It isn't only poor, dumb motorists who hate the things. The Transport Research Laboratory conducted research which showed that the stop/start driving style associated with 'traffic calming' bumps increases fuel consumption and pollution. They cause hydrocarbon emissions to rise by 70-100%, CO_2 emissions by 50-60% and CO emissions by 70-80%. It is also reckoned that the increased take-up of gas-guzzling 4x4 cars has been due in part to the fact that such high vehicles can sail over sleeping policemen with no ill effects. So these 'traffic calming' bumps are terrible for the environment, they are noisy and damage houses and cars.

So if they and we know how useless the things are, why don't council planners? Perhaps they believe that they save lives. Islington Council boasts on its website that 'Speed Humps Save Lives'. In answer to the self-posed question, 'Do speed humps affect emergency response times?' it says: 'There is no evidence to support the claim that speed humps cause delays in response times for emergency services.'

Really? Do they know better than the people running those services? As long ago as 2003, the London Ambulance Service begged councils to consider other ways to slow traffic. Its Chairman, Sigurd Reinton, said, 'The focus on reducing road deaths by cutting traffic speeds through the introduction of traffic-calming measures is well-intentioned but misplaced.' Although over the previous seven years average speeds in the capital had fallen, the number of annual road deaths had actually increased. He wanted councils to think again. 'We should be focusing on all avoidable death . . . including medical accidents such as heart attacks or cardiac arrests. Road deaths are only the tip of the iceberg.'

And why? Because while there were 280 road deaths in London annually, there were around 8,000 cardiac arrests. Ambulances were having to slow down for 'traffic calming' road bumps and other 'safety measures', even though the Ambulance Service knew well that just one minute shaved off average ambulance response times would save around 500 lives a year. In London, only 2% of those suffering the worst form of heart attack in London are revived in time, compared with 10% in some other areas. Each minute of delay in an ambulance reaching a victim reduces their chances of surviving by 10%. As Reinton concluded, 'For every life saved through traffic calming, more are lost because of ambulance delays.'

Some of those cardiac arrests are no doubt brought on by increased blood pressure among motorists navigating road humps. Is it simply idiocy or stubbornness that stops councils abandoning them and bringing in other measures? There's hope for the future, with a clever new system from Dunlop, an inflatable bump that any car which keeps to the speed limit can cross without noise or more than a tiny bump. Let's hope a growing number of councils adopt it. And if they don't, bear in mind that residents in some areas have successfully petitioned for the removal of speed bumps while some motorists have successfully sued councils over the damage to their vehicles.

How long before somebody suggests reviving the first ever traffic calming measure, the Locomotive Act of 1865, which required all cars to have somebody walk 60 yards in front waving a red flag?

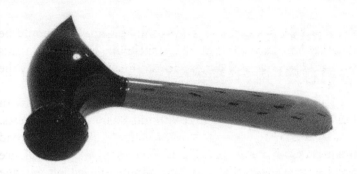

Free prize if you lose

THIS IS A PROMISE that has mushroomed in fairground booths over recent years. Knowing you cannot possibly lose, you hand over your pound, tempted by a mouthwatering array of fluffy toys, only inevitably to fail to hook a fish, throw a hoop over a watch or knock a coconut off its base.

But you haven't wasted your quid, because there's a 'Free Prize if you lose'. OK, the 'free prize' may be nothing more than an inflatable hammer that cost the stall owner only a few pence, but it's still free, right? You give him a pound, he gives you an inflatable hammer. Everyone's a winner!

From this seemingly altruistic transaction, there has now evolved a craftier version of the trick. Stalls proudly display fantastic prizes – plush teddy bears, MP3 players, bottles of spirits – adorned with signs proclaiming 'Get me free if you lose'. The 'game' is almost always a scratchcard, rather than anything that might involve skill or judgment.

Unwitting punters pay out for their scratchcard and, to their enormous surprise, find they invariably win. And the prize for winning? One of those inflatable hammers. You can see knots of bemused fairgoers leaving the stall with their inflatable hammer under their arm, baffled by the outcome. They may have 'won', but they have most definitely lost.

Just because it's called a 'fair' doesn't mean it is.

'I remember landing under sniper fire': Hillary did misspeak

POLITICIANS HAVE SUNK so low in our collective opinion that it no longer surprises us that while we elect them and pay for their salaries and perks, they think nothing of lying to us. What still has some rarity value, though, is a politician being caught out in a lie so utterly blatant and preposterous, you wonder what possessed them. After all, is a politician who can't lie well really up to the job?

One of the more splendidly jaw-dropping examples of recent years was during the 2008 Democratic elections when the Senator for New York, Hillary Clinton, went rather too far in trying to disprove her inexperience in foreign affairs (unlike Bill Clinton and domestic affairs). It was perhaps ill-advised to boast of being instrumental in bringing peace to Northern Ireland but she lost it completely in March 2008 when she talked about her visit to Bosnia in 1996. 'I remember landing under sniper fire. There was supposed to be some kind of a greeting ceremony at the airport, but instead we just ran with our heads down to get into the vehicles to get to our base.'

Why on earth did she say this? It wasn't as if it was something private that happened behind closed doors. On the contrary, she was travelling not only with her daughter Chelsea but with singer Sheryl Crow and the comedian Sinbad, both there to perform for the troops. The visit was covered extensively by the press. When some of them questioned her view of events, did she backpedal? She did not.

Yet according to the *Washington Post*'s John Pomfret, Tuzla Airport was 'one of the safest places in Bosnia' at the time. Hillary stuck to her guns. She insisted she was right. 'We came in in an evasive manoeuvre. I remember landing under sniper fire.

● *Feels like rain? Or is that sniper fire?*

There was no greeting ceremony. We ran with our heads down.
We basically were told to run to our cars.'

Unfortunately for Hillary, CBS had not decided to sell all its
old videotapes in a boot sale. They still had their news report of
that day and screened it. It showed Hillary exiting the rear of the
C-17 military transport lane in a calm unhurried way, with no
ducking of her head, even to avoid mussing her hair. Indeed, she
stopped to hear an 8-year-old Muslim girl read her a poem, after
which she kissed her.

Sinbad reckoned that the scariest part of the whole trip had
been deciding where to eat. Referring to Hillary's claim that she
was sent to such places because they were 'too dangerous' for
her President hubby, he said, 'What kind of president would say,
"Hey, man, I can't go 'cause I might get shot so I'm going to send
my wife. Oh, and take a guitar player and a comedian with you"'.

With the footage posted on YouTube for all to see, did Hillary
finally apologise for being caught out in such a bare-faced lie?
Yeah, right. That isn't her way, it isn't her husband's way and it
isn't the way for many modern politicians. Instead, Hillary had

everybody reaching for their dictionaries of archaic language when she claimed that she 'did misspeak', a word often used by Chaucer but a little less common nowadays.

Clinton claimed to have misspoken just once in 12 years, but in fact she'd begun her version of the Bosnia story three months earlier. While campaigning in Iowa in December, she had said, 'We landed in one of those corkscrew landings and ran out because they said there might be sniper fire. I don't remember anyone offering me tea on the tarmac there.' By February, she said that the greeting ceremony 'had to be moved inside because of sniper fire.'

The 'misspeak' quote itself was in an interview with the *Pittsburgh Tribune-Review*. What Hillary actually said was 'I was sleep-deprived and I misspoke'. Sleep-deprived? Unfortunate, then, that her schedule showed she'd had no public engagements at all the day before she made her gaffe and that she had slept at home that night.

If she were a child, she should have been sent to stand in the corner. Where, perhaps, her hubby might have been waiting, a man who had, after all, rewritten the dictionary when he said, 'I did not have sexual relations with that woman'. Less than a month later, Bill tried to help his wife out. 'There was a lot of fulminating because Hillary, one time late at night when she was exhausted, misstated and immediately apologized for it, what happened to her in Bosnia in 1995. Did y'all see all that? Oh, they blew it up.' Thanks a lot, Bill. It was actually in 1996, the so-called 'apology' didn't come until a week later, she'd talked about it at least five times and the occasion when she was finally caught out didn't happen late at night. It was at nine in the morning, which is why she began with the words, 'Good morning'. Unless, of course, she misspoke about that too.

In the end, the Democratic voters had clearly heard one porky too many because they misselected her.

'Butter is bad.' Says who?

THOSE RECIPES WHIPPED up by celebrity chefs may look yummy, but they could be bad for you, says a report from The Fat Panel – not a group of overlarge people, but an 'independent' group of experts in fields like diet, nutrition and public health. Many recipes they looked at had over 100% of the recommended daily intake of saturated fat in just one serving.

They were particularly infuriated by Gordon Ramsay's sticky toffee putting, which had 115% of the recommended daily amount, Phil Vickery's cottage pie with 120% and, most heinous of all, Jean-Christophe Novelli's honey roast pumpkin soup, which had a massive 216%. Other mouth-watering dishes like Nigella Lawson's egg and bacon pie and Rick Stein's raspberry cranachan also came under attack.

Reminding people of the dangers of saturated fat, the report suggested if anyone tried these recipes at home, they should make simple changes, substituting 'margarine or a vegetable oil-based spread' for the butter and cream stipulated by the celeb chefs.

But who exactly is The Fat Panel? Their website says it's 'a new, independent group which will provide objective information about the important dietary role and benefits of oils and fats.' No mention that this 'independent' body is funded by The Margarines and Spreads Association which, according to its online blurb, is made up of 'companies or firms actively engaged in the manufacture and/or sales of margarine and fat spreads in the UK'. How very independent of them.

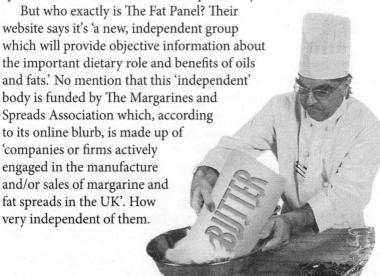

Dying in the name of harmony

THE EU CLINICAL TRIALS Directive (2001/20/EC) – stay awake at the back! – was approved in 2001. When its possible impact was raised in the UK Parliament in October 2003 after repeated warnings by experts in the field, Rosie Winterton, Minster of State at the Department of Health, assured MPs that 'the main aim of the Directive is to simplify and harmonise procedures across the Community while ensuring the protection of trial subjects and providing a safe environment for the development of new medicines.'

'Simplify', 'harmonise' and 'protect'. How splendid. According to leading practitioners, however, what the Directive, implemented in the UK in 2004, has actually done is to kill people. With red tape escalating and the whole process actually becoming more complicated and expensive, fewer patients have enrolled in clinical trials and there have been massive delays in research. Indeed, many trials that would have been held within the UK are now being held elsewhere.

6% of trials of drugs in late-stage development worldwide were carried out in the UK in 2002. That figure had dropped to 2% by 2007. In the Asia-Pacific region, however, the figure jumped from 2% to 10% in the same period.

According to Oxford epidemiologist Prof. Rory Collins, co-director of The Clinical Trial Service Unit, the legislation was all about 'ticking boxes' and took no account of the riskiness of research. Trials involving well-known drugs and treatments such as aspirin have to go through the same regulatory hoops as completely new drugs. 'If there's less activity, there's less evidence about how to treat patients safely, how to care for patients, how to save lives. The hugely increased bureaucratic burden over the last several years has made it more difficult ... I believe this is killing people.'

Professor Richard Sullivan of Kings College, London said that Cancer Research calculated that 85% more investment was needed just to keep 'business as usual'.

When the effect of the EU Clinical Trials Directive was raised in the House of Lords in February 2009, Lord Darzi of Denham, The Parliamentary Under-Secretary of State for the Department of Health, said, 'The Government are working to make the UK the best place in the world for health research ... Our national ambition (is) to double the number of patients taking part in clinical research trials in the next five years.'

There's nothing wrong with ambition, but with 35% of sites for international clinical trials in the UK now failing to recruit any patients at all, you have to wonder how realistic this target is.

The 'British' meat that comes from Thailand

LATE IN 2008, some Irish pork was discovered to contain dioxins at 200 times the permitted level. British consumers might have wished to avoid pork from Ireland. It wasn't as easy as it sounds. For there is no proper definition of 'country of origin' in either UK or European law and, no matter where the food comes from, companies can slap on a 'British' or 'Produced in Britain' label if the final product is merely processed here. So sausages, pizzas with ham topping, pork pies, sausage rolls or any ready meal might contain Irish pig meat but still say 'produced in Britain'. In fact, many of the meat products sold in Britain don't even name a country.

Unusually, the law has remained substantially unchanged since 1968. The Trades Descriptions Act states that: 'Goods shall be deemed to have been manufactured or produced in the country in which they last underwent a treatment or process resulting in a substantial change.' Meat only needs to be sliced or salted in this country for a 'produced in Britain' label to be permitted. Milk might be imported and churned here, or turkey cut into dinosaur shapes, or pork turned into bacon.

A spokesman for the Food Standards Agency confessed that: 'You could have a pie that is made in Wiltshire, for example, but uses Irish pork but it would not be labelled as such'. After worries over BSE in the early 1990s, labelling rules for beef are now more stringent. But not for pork and other animal products, even though two-thirds of imported pork is produced using animal welfare standards that would be illegal in Britain.

The FSA, which admits that 10% of our weekly shopping is probably 'counterfeit' and thus not even what it says on the labels, has issued 'guidance' saying that 'to describe a rabbit pie that is made in the UK from imported rabbit as "produced in the UK" would not be best practice.' It also says, however, that: 'It is

ultimately the responsibility of individual businesses to ensure their compliance with the law. Compliance with the advice on best practice is not required by law.'

In 2006, the FSA found that 80% of supermarket meat products didn't say where the meat originated. So a microwave chicken curry or chicken sandwich may say 'Produced in the United Kingdom' but may be made of meat which comes from intensive poultry sheds in Thailand.

Because of bird flu, imports of fresh or raw chickens from Thailand are banned, but not if they're cooked first. Or it might come from Brazil which uses chlorinated water to process birds, masking hygiene problems. Like Thailand, Brazil uses antibiotics that are forbidden here to get the birds to grow more quickly.

Aberdeen Angus steak may never have seen a Scottish field. Cumberland or Lincolnshire sausages may not actually contain British meat. A Scotch egg could be from anywhere.

Cornish pasties in Asda contain Irish beef. Somerfield sells 'Wiltshire cured bacon' from Denmark. Its spokesman said: 'The suggestion that customers automatically think the pigs are reared in Wiltshire is questionable.'

Those wanting to buy British or even ensure that fresh produce hasn't travelled half way across the globe might assume that the presence of a Union Jack would be a good indicator.

Not so. A Marks & Spencer sandwich carrying a Union Jack saying it was the 'Nation's Favourite Sandwich' revealed on the back that the corned beef was from Brazil. And Marks is one of the best supermarkets when it comes to food labelling. The only guarantee that something is British through and through is to seek out products displaying the official Quality Standard Mark.

Shadow Agriculture Minister James Paice says the system 'deceives consumers and fails British farmers', while the director of the Soil Association, Lord Melchett, regards the food labelling laws a 'complete scandal ... a fraud on the public'. But four attempts to introduce legislation on the subject since 2002 have failed, largely because they would contravene EU competition laws. In February 2009, an attempt to introduce mandatory country of origin labelling for meat and meat products was defeated, with 291 Labour MPs voting against, and only one rebel in favour.

In late 2009, Tesco – in the past a prime offender, like most of the supermarkets – decided to bow to growing pressure and became the first of the 'Big Four' supermarkets to promise to tell their customers where all the chicken, lamp and pork they sell comes from.

Something similar happens with wine. There are a few 'English' wines, made from grapes grown here. Indeed, some are superb, though pricey. There are far more 'British' wines, which are rather less expensive. But all that 'British' means is that it is fermented and bottled here, using concentrated grape juice imported in tankers. You might as well make it with a home wine kit bought in Boots.

The giraffe penis that got lost in translation

REUTERS, THE INTERNATIONAL news agency, gleefully reported the repeated theft of a Lego giraffe's penis from the Legoland Discovery Centre in Berlin.

'It's a popular souvenir,' a spokeswoman for the centre apparently confessed to the Reuters newshound. 'It's been stolen four times now.' The penis, which is made of 15,000 Lego bricks, takes a week to restore each time it's snapped off, at a cost of around 3,000 Euros. It's a great story, and is one that was picked up by newspapers around the world.

The only slight snag is that the story isn't true, as a moment's thought will verify. Do we really think the child-oriented modelmakers at Lego would have added a 12-inch phallus right at the entrance to the attraction?

The problem stems from the fact that the German word *schwanz*, meaning 'tail', is also a slang term for the male reproductive organ. And it was, indeed, the tail that had been stolen so many times.

The moral: never let an irritating fact get in the way of a good news story.

Made in China

WE'RE THE FIRST to admit that plenty of great stuff is made in China: computers, digital cameras, chicken chow mein, those little expanding paper dragons. But they also make an awful lot of crap.

China is awash with factories churning out complete rubbish. What do the underpaid, over-worked children who work godawful hours in these hell-holes imagine we *do* with all those plastic dog turds? How can they possibly comprehend a supposedly advanced Western society that pays good money (in relative terms) for such trash?

As well as the obvious garbage, though, the Chinese have cornered the market in an entirely new line of merchandise: products whose whole existence is a lie.

Here's just a single example from our local pound shop. It's a set of three magnifying glasses, billed on the packaging as 'perfect for map reading' and 'also ideal for viewing insects, leaves etc'. The trouble is, in order to save money the manufacturers have

● *Perfect for map reading?*

made the lenses out of plastic, rather than glass. And there's a very good reason why quality lenses are made of glass: it's because plastic doesn't tend to work.

Shown on the left is a photographed view through the biggest and best magnifying glass in the set. It renders the text in the dictionary beneath it utterly illegible.

So what do we expect for £1? I'll tell you what we expect: a product that's fit for the purpose for which it is sold. Being offered crap is one thing; these people are just taking the piss.

Based on a true story

IN SEARCHING FOR great stories to turn into films, Hollywood plunders not only comic books, old TV shows and earlier movie successes. It also plunders the past, often with little concern for historical accuracy. Sometimes this matters not a jot. *One Million Years B.C.* had humans and dinosaurs existing together, even though dinosaurs had been extinct for 65 million years and homo sapiens was but a twinkle in the eye of homo erectus. You don't expect a history lesson from a film with Raquel Welch in false eyelashes and a chamois leather bikini.

But many films which purport to be 'true' are still massively misleading. The worry is that their stories will come to be seen as 'real' history by moviegoers. As Dr Simon Thurley, chief executive of English Heritage, says: 'The majority of children now leave school with the sketchiest of chronology about English history. The place they turn to for that knowledge is films.' And as study published in *Psychological Science* has shown, children believe films rather than teachers or textbooks.

While praising movies such as *Mrs Brown* and *The Madness of King George*, he slammed many others, including *Robin Hood: Prince of Thieves*. 'Very, very lazy. They say "medieval" and the people automatically have to be dirty: it's very much blood and blisters and ashes and sackcloth, but, actually, people were living in multicolour then.'

One of the things that really cheeses us off, of course, is the way history is Americanised. Historian Antony Beevor, author of *Stalingrad*, declares: 'the way that Hollywood plays with national identity is completely shameless and totally irresponsible – it is a grotesque distortion of history.'

The irony is that Hollywood feels compelled to claim that these films are based on a true story. They're not interested in truth, but at the same time, they're obsessed with attaching the 'truth' label to these films, because they think it's a better way to sell them.'

Here are just a few of the more glaring inaccuracies in Hollywood movies:

Braveheart According to historian Elizabeth Ewan, the film 'almost totally sacrifices historical accuracy for epic adventure.' Among many boo-boos, supposed commoner Wallace was actually of noble descent, his father was not hanged by the British but died in a skirmish and he never met Princess Isabelle, who was nine at the time and living in France.

The Great Escape Although American POWs in Stalag Luft III did work on constructing the famous three tunnels, 'Tom', 'Dick' and 'Harry', they were moved to another part of the camp seven months before the breakout from Harry. So no Americans participated in The Great Escape at all, let alone try to escape to Switzerland on a motorbike.

Objective Burma Errol Flynn appeared to win the war in Burma virtually single-handed. The film was withdrawn in Britain after just a week in 1945 when veterans complained that there were no American troops in Burma, the campaign actually being waged by British, Indian, Australian and other Commonwealth troops. It was not shown again in Britain until 1952.

U-571 The story of how submariners captured a German Enigma machine, a crucial event in the Second World War, is fascinating. But in the film the British submarine Bulldog was American, even though the events happened in May 1941, before the United States entered the war. And, the German submarine from which the Enigma was taken was in any case U-110, not U-571, which was not captured but sunk by a flying boat in 1944. After Tony Blair agreed in the House of Commons that the movie was an 'affront' to Britain sailors, President Clinton sent a letter explaining that: 'Universal Studios has stated that the film is not intended to be an accurate portrayal of historic events.'

Saving Private Ryan The only soldiers fighting the Germans in Normandy are American, with the British are mentioned only once, in a disparaging comment about Field-Marshall Montgomery. The climactic battle with the 2nd SS 'Das Reich' Panzer Division was actually fought between the Germans and the British and Canadians, 100 miles to the East.

The Patriot Not only did the British burning of the church with women and children inside not happen, but the heroic militiaman Mel Gibson's character is based on, Francis Marion, was a racist who raped his black female slaves and hunted American Indians for sport.

Troy Characters were cremated with coins on their eyes, even though money hadn't yet been invented. Costumes were of the wrong period, and characters dallied with the wrong people and died in places very different to those recorded by Homer. As for Achilles's vaccination scar . . .

Congratulations! You've won a fabulous prize!

IT IS SAID that there is no such thing as a free lunch, but an alarming number of people seem willing to believe that there is such a thing as a free holiday, car or house. Those are the sort of prizes dangled in front of those souls who get suckered in by the free scratchcards of the type that usually fall out of glossy magazines.

You scratch the boxes and, wow, you have definitely won a prize! Indeed, it appears that everyone is a winner: all you have to do to claim your prize is make a phone call. It will only cost a pound a minute, and it won't last more than five minutes. That's not too bad, given what you're about to win.

We're not talking about the official UK Lottery scratchcards. Those are tightly supervised, and only promise what they will deliver. But the rewards for 'winners' with free scratchcards are things like two-for-one ferry tickets or mid-week breaks at holiday camps, the sort of thing being offered for free in umpteen newspapers. All the free scratchcard companies are doing is passing on the promotional vouchers that others are giving away for nothing.

It's a great business, from their point of view. They're making you pay a fiver for the privilege of 'winning' something you almost certainly don't want in the first place. Sucker in enough people and they'll be able to buy themselves a new house, a flash car and a glorious holiday.

Biometrics: the billion pound confidence trick

THE ANSWER TO almost any problem concerning terrorism, international crime, illegal immigration or identity theft over the past few years has been 'biometrics'. As Tony Blair said in 2006: 'Biometrics give us the chance to have secure identity . . . I am convinced, as are our security services, that a secure identity system will help us counter terrorism and international crime.'

Being able to identify ourselves is clearly important. However, as a Parliamentary answer in 2007 revealed, the Department for Work and Pensions has some nine million national insurance numbers it can't connect with real people. Nine million! That's 20% of the adult population.

Hence the Government's desire for a biometric identification system for passports and personal ID. Gordon Brown said in 2008 that biometrics 'will make it possible to securely link an individual to a unique identity.' But what exactly are biometrics? According to the Identity and Passport Service, they're 'unique personal characteristics, such as your fingerprints and irises.'

Using DNA isn't practical. DNA tests have to be sent to a lab and take days, which wouldn't exactly help the queues in Heathrow's immigration halls. In 2004, the UK Passport Service, as it was then, conducted a biometrics enrolment trial involving 10,000 people. In its own report, published in 2005, it declared that, when it came to fingerprinting, 'the majority of participants achieved successful verification on fingerprint'. The actual figure was only 81%. In other words, 19% had their fingerprints put into the system, which then didn't recognise them. The old-fashioned ink system works. The new method, 'flat fingerprinting', in which your fingers are scanned by a reader, doesn't.

Facial verification was even worse. That had a lamentable success rate of 69%, which dropped to 48% for disabled participants. One testing centre recorded a pass rate of just 6.25%,

● *Can you tell the difference? Airport facial scanners can't.*

and the report says operators at some centres were holding pieces
of paper over lights in an attempt to get it to work.

The rubber ring of security

You might be forgiven for thinking that the logical conclusion
would be that the technology isn't sufficiently reliable yet.
In 2006, the Commons Science and Technology Committee
urged further testing and consultation with ICT professionals.
Its advice was ignored. In August 2008, Manchester Airport's
Terminal 1 became the first international airport in the world to
put biometric scanners into operation. Home Secretary Jacqui
Smith proudly boasted that the fully-automated system would be
part of a 'ring of security' at Britain's borders. 'The UK has one
of the toughest borders in the world and we are determined to
ensure it stays that way.'

They opted to use facial recognition, perhaps because it's
twice the speed of fingerprint verification. Not only was the
technology not properly tested first but, amazingly, it was a 'live
trial'. Working on the deranged assumption that the system was
secure, the scanners were not manned by immigration officers.

Anyone with a biometric passport could avoid the queues entirely, passing through one of five unmanned gates. Only an estimated one in 20 people entering Britain through the scanners were checked by a human being.

Problems arose almost immediately. Sources in the UK Border Agency revealed that the devices could not tell if two people at a time passed through the scanners instead of one, while a UKBA worker admitted the system malfunctioned virtually every day.

A memo leaked in April 2009 contained the extraordinary information that the scanners had queried the identities of so many people that huge queues had formed. As a result, these machines were 'recalibrated', a euphemism for 'rigged to cut the queues'. According to the memo: 'Changes appear to have been made without any explanation or giving anyone a reason for the machines [allowing] what is in effect a 70% error rate ... [That] the machines do not operate at 100% is unacceptable ... The facial recognition booths are letting passengers through at 30%.' This meant that if people looked just 30% like their 'biometric' passport photo, they could enter Britain. Rob Jenkins of Glasgow University, an expert in facial recognition, said this made the system effectively useless. He made a similar recalibration to facial recognition software used at Sydney Airport and found that it could not distinguish between Gordon Brown and Mel Gibson, or even between Winona Ryder and Osama bin Laden.

80,000 people enter Britain through Manchester's Terminal 1 every day. With 20 million Britons now possessing a biometric passport and a further 50 million in the European Economic Area, you have to wonder just how strong the Manchester section of the 'ring of security' actually is. Nonetheless, the system is now being extended to include Heathrow – the busiest airport in the world.

The ultimate aim of the biometric identity system is not just to control those going in and out of Britain, but to establish everybody's identity in the UK. In a report in 2006, the Identity and Passport Service explained that ID cards would be used to prove entitlement to work and public services. With a 20% failure rate for 'flat fingerprinting' – the method used for ID cards – one in five of us, could be disadvantaged unless the technology improves drastically.

Pull my fingerprint

IT experts have shown that it is a doddle to steal biometric information, a problem that will only grow as it becomes more profitable for criminals to do so. Given the record of ministers and government offices for 'data leakage', which means Cabinet members or civil servants leaving data on public transport or losing it in the post, you have to wonder how secure the system will be for those identities it *does* recognise.

Such concerns are shrugged off because, as they keep repeating like so many self-important parrots, biometrics 'securely link an individual to a unique identity'. Those implementing the system, which is currently guesstimated to cost £5bn, believe that is the system's greatest advantage. They appear blind to the ease with which fingerprints can be duplicated.

We leave our fingerprints everywhere we go and, as researchers at Clarkson University found back in 2005, fingerprints can be lifted from virtually any surface using Play-Doh, gelatine or even a fake finger made from dental plaster. Scanners accepted 90% of their fakes as real.

If a crook is able to access your bank account using 'your' biometric data, how can you ever prove that you are the real you? Once they have it, how can you stop them using it again and again? And if a criminal or terrorist uses your biometrics for some nefarious purpose, who will the system finger for the crime? You.

Unlike an old-style passport or national insurance number, which can be cancelled and reissued, you are stuck with your fingerprints for ever. You cannot change them. Your so-called 'secure identity' will link you with the crime for the rest of your life. Be afraid. Be very afraid.

A right Titian

AT THE WORLD Economic Forum in January 2009, Gordon Brown compared himself to the artist Titian who 'reached the age of 90' and said, 'I'm finally beginning to learn how to paint.'

At Prime Minister's Questions the following month, David Cameron attacked Gordon Brown for consistently getting his facts wrong. 'You told us the other day you were like Titian aged 90. The fact is Titian died at 86.'

The real fact is, nobody knows how old Titian was when he died. He claimed he was born in 1476, though he was then 95 and probably often forgot why he'd come into a room. More recently scholars have suggested he was born some time between 1485 and 1490. What is certain is that he died on 27 August 1576. There's a death certificate.

When Cameron was speaking, Wikipedia's entry on Titian gave him 90 years on earth. Shortly afterwards, that was shaved to 86 and then somebody else amended Titian's irrefutable date of death from 1576 to 1572.

Whoever did it not only didn't realise that somebody else had just amended it, so that they were now cutting it to 82 years, but that their IP address (194.203.158.97) could be traced. Embarrassingly, it turned out that this computer was at Conservative Central Office. Oops!

Cameron said that an 'over-eager' member of staff had been disciplined and claimed he had merely been 'trying to use a light-hearted way of making the point that the Prime Minister often says things . . . that are not true'. However, he still insisted that it was 'the correct information, because I think Titian did die at 86,' making him more certain than the Louvre or the National Gallery.

Any 12-year-old could have explained how to conceal an IP address. All evidence to the contrary, Conservative HQ don't appear to employ 12-year-olds, for it's easy to ascertain that the

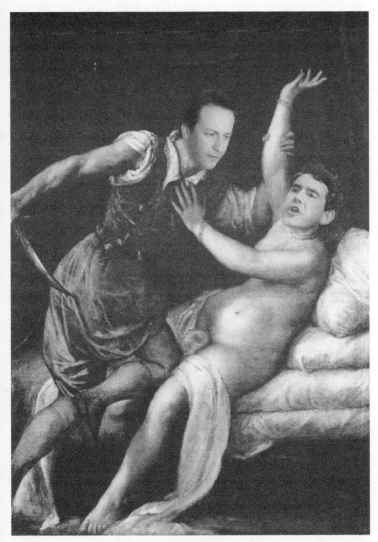

● *Cameron and Brown – with apologies to Titian.*

same IP address has not only made Wikipedia contributions on David Cameron, William Hague and Anne Widdecombe, but also Jake Gyllenhaal and the list of episodes for *American Dad*.

Wickedness on Wiki

THE ONLINE REPOSITORY of human knowledge, Wikipedia, has become an essential part of everyday life. But the secret of Wikipedia's success, relying on contributors to write the entries, is also the reason you shouldn't depend on its absolute accuracy, as teachers continually – and fruitlessly – tell their students.

When movie composer Maurice Jarre died in March 2009, many obituaries around the world quoted Jarre as saying: 'One could say my life itself has been one long soundtrack. Music was my life, music brought me to life, and music is how I will be remembered long after I leave this life. When I die there will be a final waltz playing in my head, that only I can hear.'

The only problem is, it wasn't Jarre who said this, but mischievous Irish student Shane Fitzgerald. He said he wanted to prove how journalists now use the internet as a primary source of information. As soon as he read about Jarre's death – on Wikipedia – he added the quote to the composer's entry. Although alert Wikepedia moderators removed it within minutes, Fitzgerald reposted it.

As a result, the quote appeared in obituaries in such papers as the *Independent*, the *Guardian* and the *Daily Mail*. It was only weeks later that the hoax came to light, when Fitzgerald emailed details of the hoax to the papers. Ironically, the fact that the quotation has now appeared in newspapers is adequate proof of its veracity on Wikipedia.

The nature of Wikipedia means entries are frequently tinkered with. Sometimes it's merely mischievous, sometimes it is more serious. Many alterations to the pages of American politicians came from their rivals' offices on Capitol Hill. Labour councillor David Boothroyd was found to have made unflattering amendments to David Cameron's Wikipedia entry; Liberal Democrat MP Martin Horwood discovered that his entry was subtly altered in such a way that it could harm his chances of retaining his marginal seat.

Celebrities are frequently reported to have died before their time. After this happened to Senators Robert Byrd and Edward Kennedy, Wikipedia implemented a change of policy so that amendments about living people can't go online without being checked.

Among the 'facts' reported on Wikipedia:

- Margaret Thatcher is fictitious
- Alan Titchmarsh is writing a new version of the Kama Sutra
- Robbie Williams made a living before Take That 'by eating domestic pets in pubs in and around Stoke'
- David Cameron's father bought him the Conservative Party
- Lib Dem leader Nick Clegg is a member of hip-hop outfit the Wu Tang Clan and has slept with 3,000 women
- Tony Blair had posters of Hitler on his bedroom wall as a teenager
- David Beckham was a Chinese goalkeeper in the 18th century
- The village of Denshaw near Manchester was 'home to an obese population of sun-starved, sheep hurling yokels with a brothel for a pub and a lingering tapeworm infection.'

While Wikipedia shakes its finger at online vandals, let us not forget that back in 2005, Wikipedia founder Jimmy Wales was criticised for amending his own entry. He took out references to its co-founder and downplayed his involvement with a web project that sold erotic photographs. After initially claiming the changes were only to improve the entry's accuracy, he later apologised and said: 'People shouldn't do it, including me.'

Welcome to somewhere or other

COUNCILS LOVE SPENDING our money printing handouts telling us how wonderful they are. During 2008, Birmingham Council printed up 720,000 leaflets about recycling to be pushed through the City's letterboxes.

The leaflet boasted how Birmingham had achieved its government-set recycling target of 20% a year ahead of time. Kings Norton resident Jon Cooper, however, took a moment to glance at his leaflet, which said a big 'Thank You Birmingham' to its environmentally-conscious citizens. He noticed that the skyline pictured looked unfamiliar.

A short time on Google was all it took for Mr Cooper to work out that the photograph was actually Birmingham, Alabama. Given that Birmingham, with its infamous Rotunda and distinctive new Selfridges building, has an extremely distinctive skyline, it is a little alarming that nobody at the Council noticed anything amiss. He rang them to point out their error.

Birmingham City Council, however, maintained that it was *not* an error and said that the leaflet would not be recalled or reprinted. As a Council spokesman said, 'There is no point tinkering with it. It was not a mistake. It is a generic skyline picture which is meant to symbolically represent an urban area.' Just a coincidence, then, that it showed another city that was also called Birmingham.

After the Council realised they had become a laughing stock, there was a change of tack: 'We accept that the wrong photo was used but the text and detail contained in the leaflet is wholly correct which is the most important message as we strive to further improve our green credentials . . . Birmingham is immensely proud of its recycling record and this leaflet has helped to get the recyling message across to thousands of our enthusiastic citizens.'

How is Birmingham performing against its recycling targets?

recycle

Government has set recycling targets for all local authorities. For 2007/2008 the recycling target for Birmingham is 20 %. THIS HAS ALREADY BEEN ACHIEVED A YEAR EARLY.

Thank You Birmingham!

Who do I contact for further information or to get additional recycling boxes/bags?

Contact Birmingham on:

303 1112 or email recycling@birmingham.gov.uk

What about if I have a problem or a missed collection?

Contact us using the number or email address opposite.

ContactBirmingham

0121 303 1112
www.birmingham.gov.uk
recycling@birmingham.gov.uk

● *Thank you, Birmingham! Although it seems the thanks are really due to the residents of Birmingham, Alabama.*

You do have to stop and wonder, though. If 719,999 other recipients of the leaflet didn't notice the mistake, did any of them actually look at the leaflet? And, if not, just how green is a council that can print up and distribute a stack of paper 200 feet high to no effect whatsoever?

Shock news: the politician who didn't lie after all

WOE BETIDE THE MP trying to prove they're cooler than their stuffy image, when in fact they don't know their arts from their elbow.

When Tory party leader David Cameron said in 2006 that, of the members of Girls Aloud, he most fancied Cheryl Cole, she retorted, 'Politicians know that we get listened to by more young fans than they do. That's why David Cameron said he fancied me. He was just trying to be cool. I bet he couldn't name a single song of ours. Do I fancy him? No! Politicians should stop trying to be cool and get on with running the country.'

When Hillary Clinton in 1999, still First Lady, fancied becoming a Senator for New York, she told the New York Yankees that she was a lifelong fan of the team and even popped on a baseball cap for good measure. Cue not just hilarity but much hostility among die-hard supporters. Not only had she never mentioned the team before and seemed to know nothing about them, but as someone who grew up in Chicago, she was a well-known fan of the Cubs.

Tony Blair seemed to have a similar stumble in 1997. He was reported to have told an interviewer on Radio 5 Live that, as a Newcastle United fan, his first visit to St James' Park had been 'sitting in the Gallowgate End watching Jackie Milburn'. Unfortunately, not only did the Gallowgate end not have any seating, but Milburn, Newcastle's famed centre forward, left the club in 1957.

So Blair could only have been four years old and, rather inconveniently, he was living in Australia at the time. This tale was repeated on umpteen occasions to demonstrate how untrustworthy Blair was, a man who couldn't even be trusted to tell the truth about his football team.

● *David Cameron fancies Cheryl Cole – artist's impression (come on, surely you didn't think this picture was for real?)*

It turns out, though, that Blair never said the incriminating words. Although pretty much everybody assumed he had, it wasn't until 2006 that a journalist thought to check it out. Adam Livingstone of 'Newsnight' managed to get hold of a tape.

In the interview, Blair said he'd become a Newcastle supporter 'just after Jackie Milburn'. Not only was there no mention of the Gallowgate End, but this would coincide neatly with the Blair family's return from Australia.

Sometimes politicians do tell the truth. Whose fault is it, though, if people automatically assume they're telling porkies?

Statistics, damn statistics and inflation

IT'S HUMAN NATURE for politicians to attempt to use statistics to flatter whatever argument they're spouting at any particular time. But only recently have our masters woken up to the fact that statistics can be blatantly abused to support almost any argument. How are we to judge their veracity? Most of us don't have a legion of staff trained in the arcane art of economics at our beck and call. Unless opposition politicians or the press challenge the figures, we poor dumb schmucks must simply accept what we're being told, even if our nostrils instinctively recognise a fishy smell worthy of a harbour full of dumped, rotting cod.

Of all government figures, the most important statistic is probably that for inflation. Yet the Government's manipulation of inflation numbers goes far beyond mere spin and is so outrageously and blatantly mendacious, it would see the populace of most other countries take to the barricades in anger.

Measuring the country's average cost of living is essential to set the level of pension payments and other benefits. It is a guide to how much salaries should rise if everyone isn't to get poorer. Most importantly of all, it's vital for keeping inflation in check. The new Chancellor, Gordon Brown, won almost universal approval back in 1997 for handing control of interest rates to the Bank of England, determining that they should, sensibly, be linked to the cost of living. If inflation gets out of hand, interest rates should rise to choke it back and government should not interfere with that.

But what is the cost of living? An index to measure this was first introduced during World War I, its aim to ensure workers

weren't hit by undue price rises. It comprised such essentials as meat, fish, bread, fruit, vegetables, petrol, fags and booze. Occasionally rejigged to take account of changing spending patterns, it's been in existence ever since and is now known as the Retail Prices Index. Dull it may be, but it is dependable and uncontentious.

Since 1996, there has also been a Consumer Price Index, a cost of living measure which is apparently preferred by the EU. It is a statistic of which most of us were largely unaware until, in December 2003, the Government announced that the Bank of England's inflation target would be linked to the CPI rather than the RPI in future.

Such a yawn-inducing announcement was criticised by a few alert politicians and statisticians who knew that the CPI would give a consistently lower figure than the RPI. In an instant, the Government could claim a lower inflation figure. It continued to trumpet proudly that inflation was firmly under control even though, with every passing month, more and more people realised that the published inflation figures bore no relationship to their own experience of rapidly rising living costs.

As late as March 2008, the Government claimed that inflation was only running at 2.5% per annum. But by then myth and reality were so far apart that people were looking behind the numbers. How could inflation only be at 2.5% when food and fuel prices were soaring and when utility bills and council tax had risen so sharply? In May, retail analysts Verdict Research studied a typical shopper's spending and found that fresh fruit and vegetables

had risen 16% in the year so far, as had both laundry and paper products, with canned and dried foods up 8.4%, meat and fish up 7%, while only a few things, such as pet food, had dropped. Food inflation was five or six times the official rate, while motoring costs, utility bills and the like were also soaring.

In April 2008, the *Daily Telegraph* commissioned Capital Economics to use official data to assess the rate of inflation for utility bills, food, transport, health and household maintenance. They found their Real Cost of Living Index to be 5.1%, double the official CPI rate of 2.5%.

It turns out that the CPI excludes household costs entirely. While rising fuel and food costs are in there, they are offset by ever cheaper imported clothing and high-tech gadgets, whose price is certain to fall as technology improves. Great for those who buy new TVs on a regular basis; not so great for the likes of pensioners, who might be more interested in the price of essentials such as food and housing rather than the latest must-have gadget.

The only official comment on these Alice in Wonderland figures we could find was from an unnamed spokesperson for the Office for National Statistics, who was quoted in the press. He or she said, with unhelpful candour: 'The CIP and RPI are specifically not intended to measure what people often refer to as "the cost of living".' Silly us for thinking they did.

It all went topsy turvy in late 2008, when the economy plunged over a cliff. While the CPI remained stubbornly positive, the RPI plummeted and in March 2009, became negative for the first time in 40 years. The *Telegraph*'s RCLI plunged to -10.6% in June, recovering to -7.8% in July. The cost of living going down? Not if you needed to eat. Food prices were still rising annually by 9%.

Unfit for purpose

THE CONSUMER MAGAZINE *Which?* asked its readers for examples of curious and illogical labelling, much like the sleeping pills warning that they 'may cause drowsiness' or the packets of peanuts declaring that they 'may contain nuts'. Among the more bizarre examples were:

- International Yacht Varnish. In a red tin with a ship's wheel to emphasise its nautical purpose, the small print on the back of the tin says: 'Not suitable for floors or marine use'

- A birthday card for a two-year-old made by ZZ designs with the warning: 'This card is not a toy. Not suitable for children under 3 years'

- Sainsbury's Scotch pancakes carried a photo of blueberries and the slogan: 'I love juicy blueberries.' Inside, though, are plain pancakes with no blueberries

- A box of Puma trainers: 'average contents: 2'

- A child's Superman outfit: 'Wearing of this garment does not enable you to fly'

- A domestic drill for doing DIY: 'Warning: Not intended for use as a dental drill'

- A child's scooter: 'This product moves when used'

- An office door in Pittsburgh: 'Use this door only when entering/exiting'

- Among the more confused manufacturers were Tuc crackers, whose product boasted of being 'original' and having a 'new improved recipe'.

Pride of place went to Penta for its pricey bottled water. 'You can use Penta to enjoy what we call Bio-Hydration: optimal cellular hydration that will help your body combat the negative effects of 21st century living and help your brain to stay more alert all day long.' Fortunately, the stuff also says that it is 'easy to drink'.

A load of rubbish

IN 2007, ARMS FIRMLY twisted by the Government, a rapidly growing number of local councils announced that they would in future empty residents' bins on a fortnightly basis only, rather than every week. The Government claimed that this would help meet recycling targets, as well as cut down on the mountain of rubbish sent to landfill sites. It was obviously good for us in oh-so-many ways.

But anyone with half a brain spotted the obvious flaw. If foodstuff was left to rot for a fortnight, what about the health risk? As well as the pervasive pong of *Eau de Detritus*, our rubbish could become overrun by rats, foxes, flies, seagulls, maggots and goodness knows what other vermin. Surely this would spread disease? Hell, before we knew it, the Black Death would be back with a vengeance, laying waste to swathes of . . . Well, okay, maybe not the Black Death. But surely it couldn't be sensible hanging onto decomposing food for so long? After all, as august

a body as the World Health Organisation had recommended Britain stick to weekly collections.

A DEFRA spokeswoman derided such fears. 'As long as it is combined with proper education about what to do with waste food, the new system works,' she said. This might not have assuaged everyone's fears, given DEFRA's record as the most incompetent and disaster-prone of all Government ministries. Utter the word 'DEFRA' to a farmer and you'll see that it isn't only dogs that can foam at the mouth.

Later it was discovered that advice provided by the £80 million a year quango WRAP (Waste and Resources Action Programme – clever, eh?) made it abundantly clear that the reason for moving to fortnightly collections was not to save the environment but to save money. Councils that didn't fall into line could be penalised. WRAP advised that, to reduce opposition over smells and vermin, councils should 'roll out the scheme in autumn, winter or early spring such that by the time warmer weather arrives, residents are used to the scheme and initial resistance has faded.' Councils were also advised to make any announcements about alternate weekly collection well clear of local elections so that the opposition couldn't make political capital out of it.

But what about the health issue? Fortunately Ben Bradshaw, then Minister for State at the Department for Environment, Food and Rural Affairs, was on hand to still any lingering doubts. In a written answer to a question about whether fortnightly collections would lead to a rise in flies and vermin, he said, 'There is no evidence in published studies to indicate a causal link between an increase in flies or rodents as a result of alternate week collection.'

That put us in our place. Clearly it was nobbut an old wives' tale that leaving rotting food around for two weeks would cause any health problems. Mr Bradshaw's answer clearly met with such approval from his lords and masters that he was made a

Minister of State in the Department of Health later that very month, and the number of councils switching to fortnightly collections grew to 169 out of the total of 350.

The only non-existent fly in the ointment was that there was a study about this, from the Central Science Laboratory. Commissioned by the Government in 2005 and completed the following year, it had cost £27,000 and had found that stopping weekly collections would 'significantly alter the pest infestation rates and hence the disease transmission at source', reckoning that there would indeed be an increase in 'pest species being encouraged into the home.'

Bradshaw hadn't actually lied. He had only said there was no 'published' study and, as the Government itself had decided not to publish it, he wasn't really telling porkies. In fact, nobody need have known about the study at all if it wasn't for those pesky opposition MPs and their awkward questions.

Growing numbers of people are being penalised by cash-strapped councils for falling foul of ever more complicated recycling rules:

- One 95-year-old war veteran in Norwich who put a ketchup bottle in the wrong bin had his collections stopped
- A single mum was fined £150 for putting her bins out too early
- Rubbish collectors near Warwick refused to remove a bin that had a live maggot in it, because council rules forbid them handling 'live animals'.

Mr Bradshaw was on the side of the councils, attacking people who didn't recycle properly. 'By failing to recycle,' he said, 'they are increasing their local authority's costs and therefore putting pressure on council tax bills of all the other people who are acting responsibly.' It was perhaps inevitable that journalists would examine his own rubbish. Hacks from the *Mail on Sunday* found that he'd been putting recyclable waste in with the general garbage and non-recyclable stuff in a recycling bag.

He wasn't fined, though. Odd, that.

A house with a view

FOR SALE: DETACHED fisherman's cottage in Romney Marsh, Dungeness, with three bedrooms, a garage and off-road parking. Yours for just £247,000. And as the photograph on the website of estate agents Geering & Colyer shows, it's set in the middle of lush pastures.

Except that isn't the full picture. View the cottage from the other side, and it's hard to miss the less-than-picturesque Sizewell A and B nuclear power stations looming over it, with Sizewell C due to turn up alongside in the next few years.

The estate agents' blurb mentions the cottage's location in a national nature reserve, but oddly forgets to list the convenient local electricity supplier. When pressed, a spokesman for Geering & Colyer said: 'I have no comment to make on it.'

● *Fisherman's Cottage*

We can see you!

WE ARE SPIED ON by CCTV cameras wherever we go. It is said that the average Briton is captured on a camera 300 times a day. Although we have just one per cent of the world's population, we have 20% of all its surveillance cameras. Look up and you'll see them in the street, stations, car parks and airports. There are few things more creepy than seeing one swivel to follow you as you walk, though those cameras that have microphones that listen as well as spy on us come pretty close. No wonder there are so many; a report by the House of Lords found that in the decade up to 2006, £500m was spent on installing CCTV.

The justification for all these cameras is that they reduce crime. And yet all the evidence says the effect is minimal. An internal Metropolitan Police Report – uncovered by a Freedom of Information request in August 2009 – revealed that 'for every 1,000 cameras in London, less than one crime is solved per year.' That did not prevent a Home Office spokesman responding by saying the cameras 'help communities feel safer'.

Perhaps he hadn't read the Home Office's own research which, in 2007, found that CCTV cameras had done little to cut crime other than offences involving vehicles in car parks and that up to 80% of the footage was 'far from ideal' for the Police.

He must have also missed, back in 2005, the Home Office report *Assessing the Impact of CCTV*, which found that 'CCTV cannot be deemed a success. It has cost a lot of money and it has not produced the anticipated benefits ... It would be easy to conclude from the information presented in this report that CCTV is not effective: the majority of the schemes evaluated did not reduce crime and even where there was a reduction this was mostly not due to CCTV; nor did CCTV schemes make people feel safer, much less change their behaviour.'

As for the Police, in 2008, Det Chief Inspector Mike Nevill, head of the Visual Images, Identifications and Detections Office

(VIIDO) at New Scotland Yard, told a security conference, 'CCTV was originally seen as a preventative measure ... Billions of pounds has been spent on kit, but no thought has gone into how the police are going to use the images and how they will be used in court. It's been an utter fiasco: only 3% of crimes were solved by CCTV. There's no fear of CCTV. Why don't people fear it? [They think] the cameras are not working.'

Despite all this evidence, in June 2008 Justice Minster Lord Bach told his fellow peers, 'CCTV is a powerful crime-fighting tool ... People are grateful that it is there ... Police operational experience and various research shows that it deters and detects crime and helps secure convictions. It also reduces fear of crime ... We remain committed to the use of CCTV in helping to make communities feel safer.'

So despite all the evidence that CCTV neither helps deter nor solve crime, they ignore the evidence and keep putting ever more of the bloody things up.

Who feels safer as a result? The Police, who are nice and warm staying inside watching the monitors instead of going out on the beat. And the criminals, of course.

free range and barn eggs

Picture the scene: a charming, rustic timbered structure, dust motes dancing in the rays of the sunlight filtering through the gaps in the weathered boards. A dozen hens frolic merrily among the straw, dodging the hooves of a friendly carthorse.

The reality for barn-reared and even free-range hens is rather different: the 'barn' is probably made of corrugated iron, not wood, and there will only be straw if the barn is a 'deep litter' system. The only stipulation for hens producing 'free range' eggs is that they must have daytime access to an outdoor run.

The rest of the time they can be just as tightly-packed as barn-reared birds, at a maximum density of nine per square metre of useable floor space. Imagine nine full-size hens living in a shower stall, and you start to get the idea. And with up to 16,000 hens in a single 'barn', it's not the rural idyll the name suggests.

Better than battery farming, but it's hardly an avian version of Butlins.

I wish I hadn't said that

'I have not had an affair with Petronella. It is complete balderdash. It is an inverted pyramid of piffle. It is all completely untrue and ludicrous conjecture. I am amazed people can write this drivel.'

Boris Johnson in 2004, shortly before admitting to having had an affair with Petronella Wyatt.

We can see you, part 2: how many cameras?

WHENEVER CCTV IS mentioned, it is said authoritatively that there are 4.2 million cameras in the UK, one for every 14 of us. Most newspapers use that figure, as do Government ministers and the Home Office.

But how do they know? Apparently the Information Commissioner doesn't have any figures on this, and the Government has said it doesn't even count its own cameras, let alone everyone else's.

It turns out that the number is taken from research conducted back in 2002. A couple of academics found that 49% of businesses in Putney High Street had CCTV while, in nearby Upper Richmond Road, the figure was 34%. Although the figures are very different, they simply split the difference and, using that average, assumed that, across the entire country, 41.5% of business premises would have CCTV. That would mean at least 4,285,000 CCTV cameras in Britain, which is roughly one for every 14 people.

That sounds little more than a guess to us and, what's more, a guess that was made back in 2002 when there were a hell of a lot fewer CCTV cameras than there are now.

So next time somebody grumbles about there being one camera for every 14 of us, or that there are about 4.2m cameras in total, bear in mind that no one has any idea at all how many there really are.

design and colour may vary

In other words, what you see on the packaging may not be the same as what's inside. Why not? Is the manufacturing process so uncertain that they've no idea what the finished product will look like? Do they employ colour-blind operators, who might inadvertently tip a bucket of red dye into a blue vat?

We're at a loss to understand what possible reason there could be for the item inside a box to differ from the item pictured on the outside of the box. Could it be another get-out clause: that what you think you're buying may well not be the same thing you eventually end up with? You've been conned again, but don't say they didn't warn you.

copper coins

For centuries, our coinage has been divided into three categories: gold (high value), silver (intermediate) and copper (low). Gold and silver has long been replaced as the materials of cost-effective choice, but at one time we could rely on the fact that our copper coins were, indeed, made of real copper.

Not any more: 1p and 2p pieces are now copper-plated steel. Take a magnet to one, and you'll find it sticks. We can't even trust the humble penny any more.

The small print:
Tesco on the ropes

WE'VE DISCUSSED THE MINEFIELD of small print elsewhere – but, just once in a while, the companies that try to con us with small print get their comeuppance. Such was the case with Tesco, whose 2008 pre-Christmas posters showed a glossy photograph of an iPod Nano seated in a barely-visible speaker dock at the bottom of the ad. The figures of £149.97 and £99.97 are crossed out, leaving a price tag of just £74.98.

● *What's for sale here? Not what you think*

A real Christmas bargain. Except that the iPod, featured so prominently in the ad, wasn't included in the sale: the price was for the dock only.

The iPod was shown 'for illustrative purposes only', claimed Tesco after the matter was referred to the Advertising Standards Authority. The small print, they insisted, clearly explained that the ad was just for the docking station:

Selected Discount Brands products and new price cuts available in +1500 stores. Selected UK stores. Subject to availability. Delivery charges may apply when bought online. While stocks last. Ipod not included ...

Tesco went on to insist that no customers would truly believe the iPod was included in the price, as the iPod alone would normally sell for over £100.

An almost reasonable argument, except that the crossed-out prices – suggesting the initial retail figure – would be more than enough to buy both an iPod Nano and a docking station.

Every little helps?

And now the weather

WE GLEEFULLY MOCK the astrologers and necromancers of long ago, who would examine animals' entrails for clues to what the future might hold. How different from today's shiny-suited weather forecasters, whose banks of glistening technology enable them to confidently provide an accurate prediction.

Except that, as we all know, weather forecasters do sometimes get it wrong. Spectacularly wrong. Part of the problem lies in the fact that they disagree wildly in their predictions.

We took a sample of the leading online weather sites that forecast the weather for August Bank Holiday weekend 2009. The BBC promised 'sunny intervals' on each day, with temperatures rising from 22°C on Saturday to a scorching 27°C on the Bank Holiday Monday. Weather.com expected full sun on Monday, although only offered a paltry 23°C on that day – backed up by a 0% chance of precipitation.

So why did Weather Underground claim a 30% chance of rain on Sunday, with a 20% chance of rain on Monday? Or Intellicast simply classify Monday as 'light rain'? Maybe the Met Office would be the most reliable source. Curiously, while this site predicted a mixture of sun and cloud on all three days, it made no reference to the likelihood of rain – despite describing in detail the direction, speed and gustiness of the wind.

With so many different interpretations from the raw data, we're left not knowing which one to trust. But can we assume that the predictions are generally correct?

Not according to the author of weather.slimyhorror.com, who analysed the BBC's weather predictions for over 2000 days to test the accuracy of their long-term forecasting. He found that when they were predicting just one day ahead, they averaged around 55% accuracy. Four days in advance, that figure dropped to around 37%. They got it wrong two times out of three.

But does the weather matter that much? It does if you work in the tourist industry. In Bournemouth, 25,000 potential visitors

SAT	SUN	MON
Mostly Sunny	Partly Cloudy	Sunny
High: 21°	High: 22°	High: 23°
Low: 12°	Low: 12°	Low: 14°

Saturday	Sunday	Monday
71° F | 50° F	71° F | 59° F	78° F | 59° F
22° C | 10° C	22° C | 15° C	26° C | 15° C
Clear	Chance of Rain 30% chance of precipitation	Chance of Rain 20% chance of precipitation

● *Weather from Yahoo and Wunderground: take your pick.*

cancelled their seaside plans on May Bank Holiday 2009 after a disastrous forecast predicting constant rain and thunderstorms. As it turned out, early morning rain gave way to a day of bright sunshine and a balmy 22°.

'We do suffer badly from inaccurate weather reports,' complained Bournemouth Council's tourism officer. 'It's decidedly unhelpful and costs Bournemouth millions of pounds every time they get it wrong.' The council has now installed webcams so visitors can check the true state of the local weather for themselves.

Inaccurate weather forecasts have also damaged visitor numbers in the Lincolnshire resort of Mablethorpe. Richard Borthwick, a local bar owner, grumbled in August 2009 that 'the forecast that was put out by the BBC for Wednesday said it would be heavy rain. We had brilliant sunshine. It was the best day of the year.' And so Borthwick has taken the matter into his own hands: he now organises daily forecasts on YouTube, which – he claims – have so far been 100% accurate.

So are the professional forecasters contrite in their apologies? Not a bit of it. In 2009 the Met Office – a government-owned body – paid its staff performance bonuses of over a million pounds for meeting targets and improving accuracy. This despite the April prediction of a 'barbecue summer', which fizzled out in the wettest July since records began. If anyone in another profession got it wrong as much as the forecasters do, they'd be lucky to find themselves still in a job.

Perhaps they should go back to examining entrails after all.

● *The Cottingley Fairies: a hoax that lasted nearly a lifetime.*

The camera lies: making mischief

IN 1917 TWO COUSINS, Elsie Wright (16) and Frances Griffiths (10), doctored photographs taken in their garden in Cottingley, near Bradford, that purported to show fairies dancing in the undergrowth. By today's standards, it's an obvious fake. But such was the belief in the truth of photography that the Edwardian world was fooled completely: one of the most notable believers in the Cottingley Fairies was Sir Arthur Conan Doyle, who should have known better.

It wasn't until 1981 that the two women admitted their hoax. They still insisted, however, that they really had seen fairies at the bottom of the garden.

The appearance of Photoshop has brought widespread photographic manipulation within the grasp of every internet tinkerer. It's perhaps no surprise that there have been a great many hoaxes produced for no reason other than pure mischief.

Take the case of the infamous 'Tourist Guy' image, which tugged at heartstrings worldwide. It showed a backpacker at the top of the World

● *The Tourist Guy – save your sympathy*

Trade Center, caught on a mobile phone camera, with the date '09-11-01' recorded in the corner of the frame – oblivious to the approaching airliner behind him. Was this the last moment of an innocent bystander? Not according to experts, who pointed out any number of inconsistencies in the montage, including:

- September 11 was a warm day, yet the man is shown in a wool hat and heavy coat.

- The observation deck was on the south tower. But it was the north one that was hit first – which means he must have been standing there while the other tower was ablaze.

- It's the wrong kind of plane, and it's approaching from the wrong direction.

- The observation deck was closed when the planes hit.

... and so on. But in order to provoke such a flurry of claims and counter-claims, the original image must have had a deep and profound impact on its viewers.

Bushwacked

Politicians are, naturally, prime sources of amusement when it comes to photo fakery, and George W. Bush was frequently in the firing line. Noted for his apparent lack of intelligence, malicious

● *Stupid Bush? Not quite that stupid after all.*

photo manipulators took delight in showing just how stupid the 43rd President could be. The image above shows the luckless Bush reading along on a school visit – but he's holding the book upside down. What a dork!

Well, perhaps not that much of a dork. The image is a fake. Look at the spine of his book. The publisher's logo is right at the top just as it is in the 'real' version, in the hands of the girl beside him. Whoever swapped the covers around forgot about this detail, revealing the image as a phony.

The image of Bush peering through binoculars with the lens caps still on is a trickier problem. OK, we've all inadvertently forgotten to take the lens caps off when we use binoculars at one time or another. It's just that most of us don't have the world's press standing by when we do it.

Opinion is divided as to whether this is a manipulated image or not. Certainly, there are other shots from the series that show him in the same pose with the lens caps taken off. But there could be any number of reasons why the caps would legitimately be left on: they could be night vision goggles, for instance, which would allow light to enter through a tiny pinhole during daylight.

● *Stupid Bush, again. But there could be a reason for the lens caps.*

It's not just Bush who gets lampooned in images. Even Barack Obama has come in for his fair share of mischief, such as the doctored image below apparently showing him holding a phone upside down.

These images are often taken as a bit of harmless fun. But do they do any lasting damage? Barbara Warnick, professor of Media Criticism at the University of Washington, thinks they do. 'Events have shown that parodic activity can be a consequential factor in national campaigns,' she says. In other words, people are influenced by the images even though they know them not to be true.

Or, in *other* other words: there's no smoke without fire. Fake or not, the damage is the same.

● *Obama's mystery telephone.*

• *Drive like Iggy Pop – but who insures his car?*

My favourite brand...

FEW LONDON MOTORISTS can have missed Swiftcover's striking bus-back posters for car insurance, featuring veteran punk star Iggy Pop leering out over the words 'I got insurance on my insurance'. All very well, and it's brave of Swiftcover to use such a renegade, anti-establishment figure in their promotions.

Except Iggy Pop doesn't insure his car with Swiftcover. How do we know? Because he wouldn't be allowed to. As Swiftcover's website clearly states, they decline to offer insurance to drivers working in entertainment - and that includes ageing rockers.

Swiftcover replied that they had chosen Iggy for his fast-moving lifestyle, rather than for his profession, so the nicety was irrelevant. Except surely he's known to the public more as a musician than as a fast mover? The ad was deemed misleading by the Advertising Standards Authority. And yet four months later, as we go to press, it remains plastered over the back of every other bus – albeit without the slogan.

The whole business of celebrity endorsement is a fraught area. There have been so many embarrassments and cock-ups it's hard to choose between them, but here are a few choice examples:

• When filming Tomorrow Never Dies in 1997, Pierce Brosnan requested that Bond be allowed to smoke again. The more PC producers refused, and Brosnan had to declare smoking a 'filthy habit' in the film. The real embarrassment came in Japan, where Brosnan was currently appearing in TV and print ads for Lark Japanese cigarettes.

- Eric Clapton signed a lucrative endorsement deal with Michelob beer, whose ads appeared just as Clapton went into rehab for alcoholism.

- Hertz car rental were continuing their 20-year association with O. J. Simpson when he was arrested for the murder of his wife – remember the notorious high-speed car chase footage? They certainly do at Hertz.

- Ex-Spice Girl Emma Bunton was the public face of Prego pasta sauces in 2007, just at the time when she announced she would be laying off the carbs to shed weight. Not daunted, Prego declared that she could 'have pasta sauce over meatballs or sandwiches'. Sandwiches, of course, are a notably low carb option.

- Penelope Cruz appeared in a commercial for L'Oreal Mascara, promoting their 'telescopic' product that, they claimed, made eyelashes 'up to 60% longer'. Of course, no mascara can achieve this feat. In the ad – which was slammed by the Advertising Standards Authority – Cruz was wearing false eyelashes.

Celebrity endorsements are nothing new. In the 1880s, advertisements for Vin Mariani – an alcoholic drink made from Bordeaux laced with cocaine – was promoted by none other than Pope Pius X. The drink was apparently the inspiration for Coca Cola, its two main ingredients being coca leaves and kola nuts.

- *A celebrity endorsement from . . . good grief! The Pope!*

You can't park there

IT IS ACTUALLY ILLEGAL for councils to issue parking tickets to raise money. Yet motorists could be forgiven for thinking they sometimes forget that. In 2007, a new 'fairer deal' was introduced in London with a two tier system of fines. Surprise surprise, by June 2009 councils had issued three times as many fines at the higher rate for more serious offences. As a result, £40m more was removed from motorists' pockets of motorists than the old, less fair, system would have done.

Sometimes, however, parking attendants go a little too far. The *News of the World* filmed NCP Wardens working for Westminster Council putting tickets on legally parked cars, then backing up their tickets with photographs of parking signs beside another bay entirely.

Haringey MP Lynne Featherstone parked legally in Hornsey High Street for half an hour in a bay permitting an hour's parking, only to find that she and every other motorist been issued with a ticket, despite shopkeepers pointing out the wardens' mistake. As she remarked on her blog, this from Haringay Council, already in hot water over illegal ticketing.

The website appealnow.com, which aims to help motorists fight illegal tickets, lists different ways that tickets have been wrongly issued. These include issuing tickets after a vehicle has driven away but claiming it was on the windscreen, allowing vehicles to park in bays about to be suspended, issuing tickets before the meter has expired, and – incredibly – lifting up vehicles to paint yellow lines beneath them, and then issuing tickets. All this and another 58 different examples.

What is most galling is that we shouldn't be charged for street parking at all. When parking tickets were first introduced to Britain in 1958, it was as a temporary device to raise revenue for the building of off-street car parks. In March 1959 the Earl of Gosford, for the Government, responding in the House of Lords to a sceptical questioner about this, said: 'After certain necessary prior charges . . . have been met, the surplus accruing shall be devoted to the provision and maintenance of off-street parking accommodation.'

Just a temporary measure? So was income tax.

Crazy parking ticket awards

We've heard stories of parking tickets being given to buses, cows, and even burnt-out cars. The appealnow.com website gives awards for the most amazing parking tickets, including:

- The warden who put a ticket on a rabbit hutch that had been placed briefly on the pavement outside a pet shop.
- A ticket affixed to a wrecked motorcycle while its rider, suffering a broken leg from an accident, was being lifted into an ambulance.
- Tickets given in 1995 to the cars of those people trying rescue a whale that had swum up the Thames, despite the fact that the police had given them permission to park there.

- A blood transfusion van, while donors were inside giving blood
- The Parkinson's sufferer who got a ticket for displaying his blue badge upside down.
- Four cars ticketed in a funeral procession in Westminster.

Perhaps our favourite, though, is the ticket put on a driving instructor's car when his pupil stalled doing a three-point turn.

Fool's gold

IN THE COMPETITIVE world of the Olympics, no rivalry is more intense than that between host nations to outshine all previous opening ceremonies. Beijing in 2008 was a real spectacular as viewers around the world marvelled at a series of giant footprints, made by fireworks, which strode from Tiananmen Square to the Bird's Nest Stadium.

Extremely impressive. Only almost all of it was pre-filmed computer-generated imagery. Worried that something might go wrong on the night, the Chinese spent a year creating the film, which lasted less than a minute, simulating the hazy effect of the capital's smog and even mimicking camera shake to give the impression that it was filmed from a helicopter.

At least people could marvel at the singing of 9-year-old Lin Miaoke, so pretty in her red dress and pigails. How sweet was her voice, as she sang *Hymn to the Motherland*. No wonder she became an instant star in China, giving countless interviews.

Then Chen Qigang, the musical supervisor of the ceremony, revealed she wasn't singing at all. The voice belonged to 7-year-old called Yan Peiyi, who had won a nationwide competition. She was going to perform live until a member of the Chinese politburo, watching a rehearsal, objected to her buck teeth. So photogenic Lin Miaoke was brought in to mime to a recording of Yan Peiyi.

Most people are convinced that world-renowned pianist Lang Lang wasn't playing a real piano at the ceremony either. Pianos are pretty heavy things, and tend not to bounce up and down when you thump the keys.

The truth about the age of China's gymnasts, He Kexin and Jiang Yuyuan, may never be known, although the New York Times found official Chinese records online showing that they were 14 rather than 16, the minimum age for competitors. If true, both must have been issued with fake passports to prove their eligibility.

● *We're unable to show real photographs of China's Olympic Firework spectacular, for copyright reasons. So here's a fake we knocked up in Photoshop.*

Still, at least the games were going to be a success, with all 6.8 million tickets sold in advance, unlike the lackadaisical Greeks, who only sold two-thirds of Athens' available 5.3 million tickets. Then everyone started pointing out all the empty seats at various events. So the Chinese bussed in yellow-shirted 'fans' in yellow shirts to fill seats.

Seat filling is nothing new, of course. American TV producers loathe empty seats at ceremonies, but celebrities have a tendency to wander off for a loo break or to grab a crafty fag. There's actually a company which recruits photogenic volunteers for ceremonies such as the Grammies and the MTV awards. Seat filling happens at the Oscars, too, though they use staff for work for the Academy or ABC TV.

consumers

Long gone are the days when customers would go into shops to buy things. Now consumers enter retail outlets to buy products, and it's not just the names that have changed – it's the relationship between the seller and the buyer.

We're no longer individuals who have to be wooed and tempted. We're now little more than gaping mouths that need to be filled, the possessors of credit cards that need plundering. Their job is to shift product: our job is merely to consume, and to carry on consuming until we're bloated like force-fed geese.

favourite

The website 32red.com is, its advertising tells us, 'the UK's favourite online casino and poker room.' British Airways describes itself as 'the world's favourite airline.' Does this mean they're the most popular? Or the ones that independent research has shown have the highest degree of customer satisfaction?

The word 'favourite' means nothing whatsoever, since it's in no way a value that can be quantified.

————— I wish I hadn't said that —————

'I think most people who have dealt with me, think I'm a pretty straight sort of guy, and I am.'

Tony Blair, November 1997, after the Labour Party changed its policy on tobacco advertising shortly after it accepted a £1m donation from Formula 1 supremo Bernie Ecclestone.

How low can you sync?

AMERICAN GLEE AT the Chinese Olympic fakery (see page 84 – do pay attention) turned to dust when it turned out that there was a bit of trickery involved in President Obama's inauguration.

Just before the President was sworn in, a quartet of famous classical musicians – Itzhak Perlman, Yo-Yo Ma, Anthony McGill and Gabriele Montero – played John Williams' new work *Air and Simple Gifts*.

Only they didn't. Worried that the freezing temperatures would make performing live impossibe, they pretended to play, while viewers heard a recording made two days earlier. Perlman said: 'This occasion's got to be perfect. You can't have any slip-ups.' Given the President's stumbling over his oath, perhaps they should have pre-recorded that too.

The most famous instance of lip-synching is that of Fab Morvan and Rob Pilatus, also known as *Milli Vanilli*, whose debut album sold over 14 million copies before it emerged that they weren't actually the musicians singing on it.

Elton John accused Madonna of lip-synching during her 2004 World Tour. Madonna denied it. Then she fell over on a wet stage in Rio, and, rather embarrasingly, the singing kept going, even though she didn't. Britney Spears has been roundly mocked for lip-synching badly, and Julio Iglesias's son Enrique was booed off stage in Austria when an audience realised he was miming. Even Luciano Pavarotti did it at his final performance at the 2006 Winter Olympics in Turin although, to be fair, he was extremely ill at the time.

It's happened a good deal in film musicals, of course, as was highlighted in the plot of *Singin' in the Rain*. In *My Fair Lady*, Audrey Hepburn may be Eliza Doolittle but Marni Nixon provided her singing voice. Nixon also sang for Deborah Kerr in *The King and I* and Natalie Wood in *West Side Story*, as well as providing some high notes for Marilyn Monroe's song 'Diamonds are a Girl's Best Friend' in *Gentlemen Prefer Blondes*.

free

Almost always printed in capitals, and rarely seen without its accompanying asterisk, 'FREE*' is one of the most powerful come-on words of all. It appeals to all our baser bargain-hunting instincts, and can convince even the most logical thinker that they're going to get something for nothing.

It's a word that's more often abused than just about any other. The magazine *OK!* runs a banner across its cover proudly announcing 'Two FREE magazines inside – *OK! USA* and *HOT STARS*'. In other words, the magazine has two additional sections. But are these truly two free magazines? Or just another con trick to make you think you're getting something for nothing?

In 2009 *The Observer* ran a banner headline on its front page promising 'FREE 1000 songs everyone must hear'. Except that what  they were giving away free was not the songs themselves, merely a booklet describing them.

Newspapers were taken to task by the Trading Standards Institute for making free offers on which there were terms and conditions buried deep within the publication – the problem being that because weekend papers are often shrink wrapped, it's impossible to read these terms and conditions without buying the paper first.

It's often been said that there's no such thing as a free lunch. In truth, there's no such thing as a free *anything*.

The truth about longer lasting sex

AT THE BEGINNING of 2009, London was awash with posters proclaiming 'Want Longer Lasting Sex?'. The word SEX was printed in letters often six feet high or more, prompting a flurry of complaints from mothers, teachers and Ann Widdecombe.

An 0800 phone number was provided; and, in much smaller text, the bizarre words 'nasal delivery technology'. Come again?

The offending poster was for a nasal spray designed to counter erectile dysfunction and premature ejaculation. Marketed by the Australian pharmaceutical company Advanced Medical Institute (you can call your company anything you like, of course), they offer a quick solution to a perennial problem.

In Australia, where the ads originated, the word 'sex' was forcibly covered up faster than you can say 'erectile dysfunction'. But what actually goes into this miracle cure?

The active ingredient turns out to be amomorphine, a drug more commonly used for treating Parkinson's disease. It's less potent than Viagra. The Oxford drug assessment site Bandolier reckons it's 'better than a placebo'; but Australian government agencies believe that the clinically untested and entirely unproven drug is next to useless.

Still, AMI do offer a 'money back guarantee'. But in order to qualify for the refund, patients must suffer three more rounds of treatment, including one which involves them injecting the stuff directly into their own penis. And if that's not a passion killer, we don't know what is.

Lies, damned lies, and scientific evidence

IT WASN'T THAT long ago when being an MP was a respected profession, when catching a politician in an outright lie could have harmed their career. Those were the days.

In November 2006 the Commons Science and Technology Committee published a report that effectively accused politicians of all political hues, as well as the Civil Service, of abusing scientific evidence in order to tell the most monstrous whoppers, ignoring research – even if they had commissioned it – that didn't support their argument.

Committee chairman Phil Willis recognised that many policies are enacted out of conviction, a belief that it is simply the right thing to do: 'But ministers should not disguise conviction-based policies as evidence-based.' The Committee pointed out that the absence of scientific evidence is not the same thing as the evidence of absence. In other words, just because scientists haven't yet proved something, doesn't mean it isn't the case.

One of the most notorious examples was the BSE crisis when, in December 1995, Prime Minister John Major said, 'There is currently no scientific evidence that BSE can be transmitted to humans or that eating beef causes CJD in humans.' Only three months later, after a new form of CJD had been found in 10 youngsters, Stephen Dorrell, the Health Minister, admitted, 'The most likely explanation is that these are linked to exposure to BSE before the offal ban in 1989.' Cue the collapse of the British beef industry, an export ban and something like £3.5 billion flushed down the drain. Not only did the Government not take on board existing evidence (that BSE could spread to other animals so it might be transmitted to humans) but they did not even commission research to test the extent of the problem.

In 2005 the Education and Skills Minister banned junk food and vending machines in schools. The former Chairman of the

Food Standards Agency, Sir John Krebs, complained that junk food had not even been defined, and that no cost benefit analysis had been undertaken. As an Audit Commission report pointed out, there was 'no evidence' such measures would encourage obsese kids to eat more healthily.

The Civil Service appear to be equally complicit in using and abusing scientific evidence. Criminologist Professor Tim Hope told the Committee, 'I saw our work ill-used and our faith in government's use of evidence traduced.' He talked of two case studies being contracted on burglary reduction, yet only the more favourable one was written up. The Home Office manipulated data to produce 'more favourable findings', even though it 'produces considerable distortion.' He said that at a British Society of Criminologists Conference, researchers who had been commissioned had been 'advised' by Home Office officials 'not to present their papers at the last minute even though they had been advertised in the programme.'

Reece Walters of Stirling University told the Committee, 'The Home Office is interested only in rubber-stamping the political priorities of the Government . . . to participate in Home Office research is to endorse a biased agenda.' Peter Cotgreave of the Campaign for Science & Engineering lamented the Civil Service abusing or failing to understand scientific evidence. 'This sort of cheating with scientific data is outrageous but many in the Civil Service can't tell a scientific hypothesis from an assertion or a random guess.'

And what has happened to the Commons Science and Technology Committee which dared to expose the Government's misuse of science? When the DTI and the Department for Education and Skills were split into three departments, it ceased to exist. Unfortunate, that.

serving suggestion

When a food manufacturer shows a photograph of the product on its label, the image must accurately represent the contents of the packet. But what if the manufacturer wants to display a potential use of the product, such as showing a sprig of parsley on an image of the cooked product? Surely there's some wiggle room here?

There surely is. The term 'serving suggestion' was devised precisely to allow manufacturers to include such additional items, in order to give a better impression of how the food should be served on the plate.

It wasn't long, of course, before the system began to be abused beyond recognition. It's one thing for a butter maker to show the butter spread on a piece of toast, but when we see a tub of bicarbonate of soda displaying gingerbread men as a 'serving suggestion', we know the phrase has become ludicrous.

—————— I wish I hadn't said that ——————

'A day like today is not a day for soundbites, really. But I feel the hand of history upon our shoulders. I really do.'

Tony Blair, April 1998, during the negotiations leading to the Good Friday agreement.

Good Service

IF YOU HAVE TO TRAVEL on the London Underground, you'll know that they've taken to sticking up boards with smug little signs beside the list of their lines, invariably saying 'Good Service'. For the record, this is London Underground's 'Terminology explained':

- *Good service: No noticeable impact on your journey.*
- *Minor delays: Noticeably longer journey time, however stay with your planned route.*
- *Severe delays: Significantly longer journey time – consider using another route.*
- *Suspended/Part suspended: Your planned route is unavailable – please use another route or mode of transport.*

So it's a 'good service' even if you freeze your nuts off for 20 minutes at 11 o'clock at night at Earl's Court waiting for a Wimbledon train, puzzling why three trains have just gone to Olympia even though the exhibition hall closed hours ago. It's a good service even if the escalator is being repaired and you have to lug your suitcase up it. It's a good service when you've been stuck for five minutes between stations in a stifling carriage with an Australian's backpack pushing your nose into somebody's armpit. It's a good service if you are ignored or patronised by the officious and inefficient staff. It's a good service that doesn't have air conditioning, that is strewn with rubbish, that is infested with rats and that does nothing to stop people eating their appallingly smelly junk food. It's a good service that drives those who are compelled to use it to utter distraction.

As they keep reminding us, we are the 'customers'. Isn't it up to *us* to decide whether it's a good service or not? If we get good service from other businesses, there's an accepted way of acknowledging it. When was the last time you heard of somebody tipping a member of staff on the London Underground?

No more boom and bust

POLITICIANS WHO BEND with the prevailing wind fervently hope that we can't recall what they said just a few months before. As most of what they say goes in one ear and out the other, we usually can't. Sometimes, however, their attempts to pretend they didn't say what we know full well they *did* say have all the success of a giant bellyflop echoing from the swimming pool of life.

In October 2008, as the 'Credit Crunch' rather than 'the worst economic crisis since the 1930s' was biting, Allison Pearson interviewed Gordon Brown for the *Daily Mail* and asked if he any regrets about his boast: 'No more boom and bust.'

Brown insisted he'd said no such thing. 'I actually said, "No more *Tory* boom and bust",' he replied. As if *Labour* boom and bust was somehow more palatable. So what did he actually say? These are a few of the quotes he was only too happy to utter:

'I am satisfied that the new monetary policy arrangements will deliver long-term price stability, and prevent a return to the cycle of boom and bust.'   *November 1997*

'The Government have put in place policies to deliver that objective and are determined to avoid a return to boom and bust.'   *May 1998*

'Rigorous financial discipline that, together with monetary stability, ends once and for all the boom and bust that for 30 years has undermined stability.'   *June 1998*

'A framework to secure long-term economic stability and put an end to the damaging cycle of boom and bust.' *CBI Dinner, 18 May 1999*

'Under this Government, Britain will not return to the boom and bust of the past.'
Pre-Budget Report, 9 November 1999

'Indeed, Britain was set to repeat the old, familiar cycle of boom and bust.'
November 1999

'Britain does not want a return to boom and bust.'
Budget Statement, 21 March 2000

'Our first task has been to escape from 18 years of boom and bust and to never go back . . . Such short termism is the old way that brought us the stop go, boom bust economy, the ups and downs, of the past and this I will not endorse.'
TUC Congress, 12 September 2000

'So our approach is to reject the old vicious circle of the... old boom and bust.'
Pre-Budget Report, 8 November 2000

'Mr Deputy Speaker, we will not return to boom and bust.'
Budget Statement, 7 March 2001

'As I have said before Mr Deputy Speaker: No return to boom and bust.'
Budget Statement, 22 March 2006

'Boom and bust is a term that applied to the Conservative years and two of the worst recessions in history.'
December 2006

'And we will never return to the old boom and bust.'
Budget Statement, 21 March 2007

Many of Mr Brown's colleagues, and even his predecessor, did link the phrase to the Tories, however. Here are a few of them . . .

'Examine the legacy that we inherited and what we did. We had boom-and-bust economics and a doubled national debt.'
Tony Blair, November 1998

'We have the best chance of ending boom and bust in years.'
Tony Blair, November 1999

'The Government have rejected the boom and bust of the Conservative party.' *Tony Blair, 2000 Conference*

'In the first two terms we corrected the weaknesses of the Tory years: boom-and-bust economics.'
Tony Blair, 2005 Conference

'In 1997, we faced daunting challenges. Boom and bust economics . . . Now, for all that remains to be done, dwell for a moment on what has been achieved.'
Tony Blair, 2006 Conference

'We have a healthy and stable economy and an end to the boom and bust that characterised the Tory years.' *Alistair Darling, January 2000*

'The Government's first priority on coming to office was to secure long-term economic stability and put an end to the damaging cycle of boom and bust.'
Alan Johnson, February 2000

'We must avoid a return to the days of boom and bust that manufacturers had to endure for a long time under the Conservatives.'
Ruth Kelly, May 2002

'We know that they want to turn the clock back, but it would be foolish to turn it back to a policy of boom and bust.' *Yvette Cooper, May 2004*

'Labour economic stability has replaced Tory boom and bust.'
John Prescott, January 2005

Show homes: the tricks they use to make us buy

Every time a new housing development goes up, the first house to be completed is the 'show home' – a bright, airy, typically furnished house that shows the prospective buyer exactly what they'll be spending their cash on.

Except that what you see in these show homes is often a series of cunning tricks designed to fool you into thinking the houses are bigger and better than they really are. Catriona Bright, director of the New Build Inspections website, points out: 'A significant number of owners of properties we inspect are disappointed their home is a pale reflection of the show homes that they are shown.'

Among the tricks used by unscrupulous developers are:

- Leaving all the lights on. This gives the impression that the house is airy and full of natural light, and helps conceal the fact that bathrooms may not have windows.

- Removing internal doors. The effect is to make the rooms appear bigger.

- Fitting the house with lots of mirrors and glass furniture. Again, the house looks bigger, and light passes through it more effectively.

- Using children's furniture in rooms, as well as furniture such as cupboards and sideboards that are only half the depth of the real thing. Again, this makes the rooms look much bigger than they really are.

- Using top quality fixtures, generally far superior to those found in the real sale houses.

- Fitting out bedrooms with just a bed and a bedside table. Only the more observant visitors will notice that there's no chest of drawers or wardrobe.

- Professionally landscaping gardens to a much higher standard than the basic turf specified for the rest of the development.

- Turning central heating up very high. It's not for the comfort of the visitor, but actively to discourage them from loitering too long. The longer they're there, the more discrepancies they'll notice.

As if this weren't bad enough, buyers of new homes are frequently victims of 'snagging' – the appearance of defects after the house has been built (and paid for). A Review of Housing Supply research document commissioned by the Government shows that an astonishing 90% of home owners experience defects in their houses; a survey by Zurich Insurance goes on to show that nearly 70% of buyers found the defects had not been remedied by the time they moved into the properties.

The number of snags depends largely on the size of the house. Buyers of a one-bedroom house can expect at least 40 defects; those buying four-bedroom properties are likely to discover over 130 faults.

The final word, from Catriona Bright: 'The show home will have been finished to the highest specifications, possibly by contractors different from those building your home, which you have bought off-plan and have not even seen. Unlike the show home, your property may be uninhabitable when you first move in, but once the contract is signed it is watertight and there is no going back.'

free delivery

Pizza outlets were the first fast food companies to offer free delivery. It made sense: pizzas are flat, easily transportable, and the cost of raw materials is minimal – so they could afford to employ a string of adolescent moped riders with L plates and only a tenuous geographic knowledge of the immediate area. The idea was so successful that other types of takeaway started getting in on the act.

But look closely at any one of the dozen or more Indian or Chinese takeaway leaflets that come through your letterbox in a week: beneath 'free delivery' there's often the additional notice: '10% off if you collect'. Wow! Double generosity! Or is it that they've simply added that 10% to the menu prices as a covert delivery charge?

only

The word 'only' used to indicate that a price was unusually low. But flip through a typical store catalogue and you'll see the word sprinkled liberally throughout the pricing, so that just about every price is listed as 'only' – whether it's a pen at 'only 99p' or a car at 'only £8,999'. The word has become so debased it's now utterly meaningless.

The time now is precisely… er…

BBC RADIO HAS been broadcasting 'pips' leading up to the hour since 1924. And they've been bang-on accurate ever since – but now that accuracy is threatened by, of all things, digital radio.

The problem is that the broadcast sound takes a couple of seconds longer to emerge from a digital radio than it does its analogue counterpart. The delay is brought about by the fact that it takes around a second for the signal to be encoded before transmission, and then another second for the listener's radio to decode it. So while old-fashioned radios may be spot on, those with cutting-edge digital devices will find themselves a couple of seconds out of date. Listen to the radio online on your computer, and it will be at a different time again.

So why don't the BBC just broadcast the pips a couple of seconds earlier? Two reasons. First, because then listeners with analogue sets would be getting them at the wrong time. And second, because although a radio may take around a second to decode the signal, it's not exactly a second: different radios decode the signal at different rates.

Historical note: the pips were generated originally by a super-accurate clock at the Royal Observatory, Greenwich, and was intended to spread the use of Greenwich Mean Time around the civilised world. Since the Royal Observatory moved to the Canary Islands in 1990, however, the BBC has faked the signal with its own pips.

Pip pip!

Your call is important to us – it's worth millions

'**WHICH 32-YEAR-OLD MODEL** celebrated her birthday at the weekend? Kate Moss, Jerry Hall, or Twiggy? If you think you know the answer, ring this number.' Tough, brain-wracking TV phone-in quizzes like this, encouraging people to pay premium rates, always seemed a disgraceful rip-off. We didn't realise how much of a rip-off.

Late night interactive quizzes, shows like *Quiz Call*, *Quiz Mania* and *The Mint* made a fortune for the independent TV companies. ITV Play made £9m in just six months from these tatty shows, which encouraged viewers to think that the answers would be simple and the prizes immense.

Although it seemed obvious that viewers were being fleeced, the authorities turned a blind eye. Only when *The Sunday Times* discovered that *Quiz Call* had charged thousands of callers 75p, while simultaneously blocking them from answering the prize question, did MPs question what was going on, forcing Ofcom to act.

In changing the guidelines in January 2007, Ofcom revealed that viewers had been quizzed about things found in a woman's handbag. The answers included 'balaclava' and 'rawl plugs'. A question about 'Things in Australia' had an answer 'Alice *******', which turned out to be not just 'Alice Springs' but 'Alice Springs Camel Cup', despite the evidence of precisely seven asterisks.

In upturning the phone-in dustbin, all other sorts of nasty things came to light:

- Callers to *The X Factor* were found to have been overcharged £200,000 because of a computer error.
- Competition winners on Channel 5's *Brainteaser* were faked.
- Callers paid £1.80 to enter GMTV quizzes, after the finalists

list had been compiled. It was alleged that GMTV had rooked viewers out of millions of pounds. The company was fined £2m.

Viewers to ITV quizzes that were repeats were not told that they weren't live, and so had no chance of winning.

An audit discovered that millions of ITV viewers had been conned. Callers were being charged millions of pounds on shows, even though voting had finished. On other shows, producers ignored the voting and made their own choices of the winners. Programmes involved included *Ant and Dec's Gameshow Marathon* and *Saturday Night Takeaway, Soapstar Superstar* and *The X Factor*, where 14% of votes for the 2005

X Factor final were not counted, though those callers were still charged £900,000.

- *The Richard and Judy Show* was fined a record £150,000 for misleading viewers on its *You Say, We Pay* quiz, apparently improperly making revenue of £2.2m.
- Shock, horror. *Blue Peter* was found to have misled its audience. Children voted to call a new cat Cookie, but the producers opted for Socks instead. On another occasion, they made a visiting child pose as a competition winner.
- Even the BBC's charity phone-ins for *Comic Relief* and *Children in Need* were discovered to have faked their competition winners.
- The BBC was revealed to have fiddled competition winners on a range of shows, ignored voting results and encouraged people to vote even if voting had closed or they stood no chance of winning. On *The Liz Kershaw Show*, the production team themselves, and their friends, posed as competition callers.

In total, the BBC had to pay fines of £545,000, money that of course also comes from the public, only this time through their licence fees.

On the very day that ITV was fined a record £5.67m by Ofcom over the scandal came the revelation that producers had fiddled the results of the *British Comedy Awards* in 2005. Although Catherine Tate had won the People's Choice Award, the producers had – to guarantee his attendance – promised Robbie Williams he could give a prize to Ant and Dec. The People's Choice award was the only one still to be decided, so Catherine Tate's name was scratched out.

With advertising revenue falling dramatically, the loss to the independent TV stations of the money from phone-ins was severe. ITV reckoned that the scandal cost it £18m, though that doesn't include future revenue they now won't get. 'Which organ did the broadcasters shoot themselves in? The foot, the arse or the elbow? If you think you know the answer, don't ring us.'

A load of pollocks

WE CONFESS WE'D NEVER heard of pollock, the fish, until a while ago. Heavily used in making fish fingers in recent years thanks to the overfishing of cod, it apparently has a similar taste but is less endangered. Pollock, however, has long had a downmarket reputation as a food fit only for cats, hence the saying 'Pollock for puss, coley for the cat'. It was sometimes found to have been substituted for cod by unscrupulous fish and chip shops.

Sainsbury's, however, reckoned that the problem wasn't the fish itself, but its name, believing that customers were too embarrassed to ask for it – even though the supermarket chain preferred to spell it 'Pollack'. So, in April 2009, they rebranded it, selling it in special packaging reminiscent of the American artist Jackson Pollock while changing its name, rather bizarrely, to 'colin' – the French name for hake.

Sales of the fish in Sainsbury's went up by 50%. In September, presumably also helped by recession belt-tightening, seafood-promoting quango Seafish announced in September that pollock – or colin – had jumped into the fish hit parade at No. 8, outselling trout and scampi combined.

It isn't the first instance of fish rebranding, of course. How much rock salmon or huss would be sold if fish and chip shops had stuck to the old name – dogfish?

Faking it big time

HOW APPROPRIATE THAT the successful TV series *Faking It* was made by RDF, for it was RDF who, in 2007, made the documentary *A Year with the Queen* and, to sex it up, made a trailer that showed the Queen storming out of a photographic session with Annie Leibovitz in a huff. The BBC, scenting a ratings winner, broadcast the trailer repeatedly before somebody pointed out that the shot of her walking out was actually filmed *before* the session, and that the trailer massively misrepresented what had happened.

The newspaper wolves went out for blood. Never ever, ever guilty of faking a story themselves, of course, the press went sniffing for any sort of fakery in TV. And boy, did they find it.

- An ITV documentary trumpeted in its publicity that it depicted the actual death of an Alzheimer's sufferer. In fact, he went into a coma and died three days later.

- In *The F Word*, Gordon Ramsay appeared to have caught several sea bass. It transpired that an expert spearfisherman had caught them earlier.

- In a BBC TV news report about quintuplets born to a Russian woman, the sound of babies crying was added, even though they were on respirators.

- Sky's *Brainiac* faked explosions in scientific experiments because they felt the real reactions didn't look spectacular enough.

- Channel 4's series *Dumped* purported to show a group of people trying to live on a rubbish dump. However, it was later revealed that health and safety considerations meant they couldn't use a real dump but had to build their own.

- In Wilderness expert Bear Grylls's series 'Born Survivor', he didn't suffer quite as much as it appeared to viewers. Although Britain's youngest conqueror of Everest did bite off a snake's head for breakfast in California's Sierra Nevada, he and the crew stayed some nights at The Pines Resort at Bass Lake, a 'cosy getaway for families' with roaring fires, hot tubs and internet access. Grylls claimed to lassoo a wild mustang, saying that, 'This is one of the few places in the whole of the U.S. where horses still roam wild.' Maybe they do, but these were trekking horses and were probably only wild because they had been taken there by trailer.

A survival consultant who advised the programme said that while Grylls was supposed to live in one episode like a 'real-life Robinson Crusoe', the supposed 'desert island' was actually in the Hawaii archipelago. The consultant claimed that he was in charge of a team of builders who made a Polynesian-style raft which was then taken apart so Grylls could make it again on camera. When filming on Mount Kilauea, a live volcano, the poisonous sulphur dioxide didn't show on camera. So the production crew faked it with smoke generators and used burning hot coals to simulate molten magma.

Silliest of all the TV fakery was when it was claimed – in a supposed scandal nicknamed *Noddygate* – that the BBC's creative director, Alan Yentob, wasn't even present at some interviews for his arts series *Imagine*, even though he was seen nodding away as if in response to something the interviewee said. Later it transpired that no 'noddy shots' of Yentob *had* appeared in *Imagine*. But by then Channel 5 News and most other news programmes had banned noddy shots, replacing them with ridiculous cutaways which 'prove' the interviewers are actually there.

TV producers may be trying to show that they're being more honest, but we should still maintain a healthy scepticism. After all, if 'reality tv' shows purport to show us true life, why do all these shows employ scriptwriters?

A famine by any other name

IN 2005, BBC TV NEWS, followed by many other outlets around the world, carried reports about a disastrous famine in Niger. One third of the population were said to be starving: 'This is the only part of Niger where anyone has even tried to estimate how many people have starved to death,' said its reporter, 'and the indications are that just in this town and and the villages immediately surrounding it, thousands of people have died in the last few months.' The reports were backed by the UN and the chief of its humanitarian division, Jan Egeland.

A documentary team from Norway's TV2 channel, the country's largest commercial broadcaster, went to Niger intending to make a film about the aid that flooded into the country in the wake of the news reports. To their surprise, they couldn't find anyone who knew anything about the famine. There was malnutrition and disease but 'there was no one who had heard of anyone dying from the famine of 2005,' said producer Mats Ektvedt.

They interviewed Niger's prime minister, local farmers and people working in assorted aid programmes. One local woman is quoted in their documentary saying 'I've never heard of anyone starving to death here. It was tough, but I never saw anyone die of hunger.' The previous year did not see a plague of locusts or a drought, either of which might have caused a famine.

Esther Garvi, who has lived in Niger since she was six and whose family have run the Eden Programme there for 20 years, supporting local agriculture, says, 'To this day, I have yet to meet one person in the whole of Niger who knows of any person who died from not having food to eat. I know many people who have died from diseases and accidents, but in a hospitable country like Niger, I know of no one who would leave anyone to starve to death.'

The food aid which arrived in the area in fact caused more problems, as it undermined the ability of local farmers to provide food for the local population. Those children who were said to be dying of malnutrition were in reality suffering from diarrhoea or malaria, but the aid was not targeted at combatting disease.

Anneli Eriksson, a nurse with Doctors Without Borders at the time, while not criticising the BBC's coverage, said: 'The reporting seemed very one-dimensional. It's either there are no problems or there is a major famine. Clearly, when there is a crisis, reporting can get a bit inflated.'

When Egeland was interviewed for the documentary, at one point he says, 'Why was there no famine? Because the BBC and I sounded the alarm!' Later, queried on whether there was a famine or not, he hesitates, says there are different ways to define a famine, then insists, 'Yes, there was a famine.'

The documentary, *Famine Scam*, which criticises both the BBC and the United Nations, won third prize in the Monte Carlo TV Festival in 2008. The BBC's response? To withdraw permission for the use of its footage, blocking the documentary's international release, even though TV2 had bought the broadcast rights. In a statement to the Swedish broadcaster SVT, reported in *The Guardian*, the BBC said: 'BBC News refuted the TV2 allegations unequivocally and we absolutely stand by the validity and professionalism of Hilary Anderson's reports.'

Without the BBC footage, the documentary is not as powerful as the version that was shown at the Monte Carlo TV Festival. But the unedited *Famine Scam* is available to view online at YouTube and elsewhere.

Honeytokens, Nihilartikels and Mountweazels

THE 1975 EDITION of the *New Columbia Encyclopedia* carried a biography of Lillian Virginia Mountweazel, the fountain designer turned photographer who took pictures of mailboxes and who died, tragically, at the age of just 31 in an explosion during an assignment for *Combustibles* magazine.

But you shouldn't shed too many tears for the unfortunate Miss Mountweazel. She never existed. She was the subject of a made-up article the encyclopedia's publishers invented in order to trap plagiarists, who might try to steal their information and pass it off as their own. 'Mountweazel' has now entered the dictionary as a noun for these made-up copyright traps.

Including made-up facts in reference books is a tradition that goes back a long way. The German *Psychyrembel Klinisches Wörtebuch*, for instance, included an entry to the 'steinlaus', an imaginary rock-eating louse. The 1980 edition of the *New Grove Dictionary of Music* features an entry for the composer Esrum-Hellerup – who never existed.

Map publishers frequently include fictitious streets, usually just outside the core area of the map's coverage, to be used as proof if another publisher uses their map as reference without walking the streets to map the area themselves. The A-Z company, for instance, has a policy of giving fictitious names to streets on new developments that have not yet been named – Lye Close in Bristol is one such example.

Sometimes the scheme is so successful that the name moves from fiction into reality. Otto G. Lindberg and Ernest Alpers, mapping a dirt-road intersection in the Catskills in the 1930s for the General Drafting Company, included a settlement they named 'Agloe', an anagram of their initials. When a shopkeeper later built a store on the site, he was given the name of the locality by the local county administrators – who, naturally enough, found it on their map. And so before long the Agloe General Store proudly opened its doors.

Even dictionary compilers occasionally play fast and loose with the truth. When it emerged that the new edition of the *New Oxford American Dictionary* included a made-up word beginning with the letter 'e', lexicographers vied to find the culprit. One investigator identified six possible Mountweazels, including 'eurocreep' (the gradual acceptance of the Euro as currency) and 'ELSS' (an abbreviation for Extravehicular Life Support System). The problem is, it's fiendishly hard to say for certain that a particular word doesn't exist. The consensus is that the fake word was 'Esquivalience', purportedly a 19th century term for 'the willful avoidance of one's official responsibilities'.

Those working in computer security will often include 'honeytokens', deliberately fictitious database entries designed as traps. These might be email addresses, which will clearly show if a mailing list has been stolen or sold on. The trick is to find a honeytoken which is good enough to withstand scrutiny, but which will not cause problems if taken to be real by the very people it is there to protect.

Another word for honeytokens and Mountweazels is 'nihilartikels', a combination of two German words meaning 'nothing article'. But it seems this word might itself be nothing more than a nihilartikel: it is believed that this word was made up by a contributor to the German version of Wikipedia. Just who can you trust these days?

109

Why you can't just pop in for a pint of milk

HAVE YOU EVER TRIED dashing into a supermarket for something simple and found yourself emerging, some time later, with a trolley groaning with stuff you hadn't realised you wanted or needed? Foolish person. You are pitting yourself against some of the finest minds in retailing whose sole aim is to make you, the consumer, spend as much money as possible.

It's the same with shopping centres. These are designed, not as you might expect, to make shoppers feel comfortable and content but, on the contrary, to disorient and confuse them. They aim to induce a condition known as the 'Gruen transfer', named after the designer of the first shopping mall in 1856.

The Gruen transfer is the moment when customers suffer 'scripted disorientation'. They slow from a confident stride – fully aware of what they have come to buy – to a baffled dawdle, eyes glazing over as they realise there's so much more on offer than they imagined. If you ever find yourself lost in one of these places, it's not that you have no sense of direction, but that they have succeeded in their object of bamboozling you.

● *Two pasta ingredients side by side. But where the tortellini are priced per kg, the costlier cappelletti is per 100g, making comparison difficult.*

It isn't just your eyes they play tricks with. They also use ambient sounds and music to slow you down and tempt you to spend money. Anyone who has ever shopped at IKEA will realise how difficult it is to find and buy just one item, as you are led involuntarily past every product in the store. What retailers want are not alert shoppers, but lobotomised zombies.

Such psychological tricks have been used on us for sixty years or more. Indeed, in the early days of the Muzak corporation – notorious for infuriating people in lifts the world over – the company employed psychologists to research how music could be used to increase workers' productivity. Using their 'Stimulus Progression' technique, workers' 'fatigue curves' were overcome while, under the influence of Muzak, shoppers spent more than they did in silent stores. No wonder Muzak was heard almost everywhere we went.

Retailers use a variety of tricks to encourage us to spend more on products we had no intention of buying when we entered their stores. These include:

- Moving successive escalators so we have to walk around the floor to find the next route up. On the way, of course, you pass a variety of tempting purchases.

- Placing mirrors everywhere in department stores, which slow shoppers down. You'll rarely see a window to remind you there's a world outside, however.

- In department stores, over the past few years, straight lines have been outlawed. Why let your customers go immediately to the department they want when you can lead them around umpteen tempting displays? Uses more shoe leather, too, which is good news for the footwear department.

- Placing essential items such as milk, bread and eggs as far as possible from the entrance. Supermarkets are fully aware that these are 'need to buy' items, making you pass aisles of groaning shelves to get to them, increasing the chances of you making further impulse purchases along the way. Other low margin staples will be tucked away in some hard to locate place, so you have to trawl the store to find them.

- Placing fruit and veg near the entrance, because these are thought to give customers a feeling of happiness and health, and rev them up to spend more.

- Placing regular-priced items in bins at aisle ends, so they resemble 'bargain bins' – even though they aren't.

- Positioning high profit margin items at eye level. If you're trying to save money, make sure you bend down to look at the lower shelves.

- Wafting the smell of freshly baked bread at all times of day to make you feel hungry, even though the actual baking probably finished hours before.

- Changing layouts to move regularly purchased items around. If something isn't where you expect to find it, you have to pass a lot more products before you track it down.

- Deliberately confusing unit prices to prevent shoppers from making accurate comparisons. Similar items are often priced by weight for one commodity, and by volume for another

- Pricing luxury items 'per 100g' rather than 'per kg' so you don't realise how much they really cost.

- Adding 'weasel' words to packaging such as 'value' and 'essential' which mean absolutely nothing out of context. In Sainsbury's, for instance, own-brand blended whisky is actually least expensive if you buy a litre. Buy 70cl or 1.5l and you're paying more per litre.

Tinned items such as fish and vegetables, which tend to include a quantity of water or oil, are routinely displayed with two weights: the weight of the whole contents, and a second figure mysteriously labelled 'gdr.wt'.

Nowhere in the store is it explained that this abbreviation stands for 'grammes drained net weight' – in other words, the weight of the commodity you actually want, as opposed to the added liquid necessary for freshness in the packaging.

It may not seem like a huge difference, but it makes it almost impossible for the average shopper to compare prices accurately. And while Tesco uses the 'dgr.wt' system, Sainsbury's often merely places an asterisk next to the true content figure.

Often, we'll find that the price shown per 100g (or whatever unit is used) bears little relation to the unit cost of the item we're buying, as is the case with the third tuna example on this page. Now, we're not suggesting that Tesco are deliberately setting out to mislead us here – but if they're not, then they're certainly displaying a level of mathematical incompetence that we would not expect from Britain's major retailer.

As far as we're aware, no British supermarket has

● Two tins of tuna in Tesco, all priced at £1.44. Only the 'gdr.wt' figure shows that we're getting more actual tuna packed in oil than we do when packed in brine.

● Tuna again: £1.44 for 200g, or 96p per 100g. At least one of these figures must be grossly erroneous.

yet resorted to a trick employed by one American chain, who painted a child's hopscotch game on the floor right beside all those 'can we have?' cereals.

The lesson seems to be: make sure you eat before you shop, so that you're not hungry; take a detailed list; and have a calculator handy. And a GCSE in maths wouldn't go amiss.

Watt's the fuss about?

IN ACCORDANCE WITH EU law, we have to switch from heat-wasting incandescent light bulbs to new-style CFL (compact fluorescent) bulbs. Cue lots of grumbling from people who find that they aren't as bright, that they give out a dull light which muddies colours and that they take ages to reach their maximum brightness.

But our eyes must be deceiving us, say Government ministers and their lackeys. On the eve of the switch, Environment Minister Dan Norris wrote to a newspaper: 'Most low-energy bulbs come on immediately and all have a mandatory maximum warm-up time of two seconds.' That's telling German Chancellor Angela Merkel then. She admitted at the EU summit which ordered the switchover that: 'They're not yet quite bright enough. When I'm looking for something I've dropped on the carpet, I have a bit of a problem.'

So are we all wrong then? Perhaps not. The EU's own website on CFLs is more honest than our own government's. 'Currently, exaggerated claims are often made on the packaging about the light output of compact fluorescent lamps (e.g. that a 11-12 Watt compact fluorescent lamp would be the equivalent of a 60 Watt incandescent, which is not true).'

As the gradual banning of incandescent bulbs began in September 2009, the *Sunday Telegraph* tested a variety of bulbs. It found that old-style clear bulbs gave out around 120 lux of illumination and the frosted variety about 100 lux. By comparison, even allowing (a supposedly unnecessary) 10 minutes to warm up, the best 11W energy-saving bulb, the claimed equivalent, gave out 79 lux and the worst only 60 lux, making it just half as bright as the bulb it was supposed to replace.

In telling us what we know to be untrue, the Government makes us doubt every other 'fact' about them. Maybe they won't last as long as claimed and maybe the mercury they contain (banned in so many other things) will poison our

seas when they're disposed of, which of course can only be done at official sites. Many people admit to leaving some on constantly, wasting energy, because they know they *don't* come on instantly. If it's very cold, they hardly come on at all. Most manufacturers don't warn that CFLs shouldn't be used in bathrooms or inside sealed light fittings. As for the mercury, it may be safe for the user, but how long before the first documentary shows the appalling safety conditions for the poor sods manufacturing them in China?

● *11 new Watts = 60 old Watts? Oh no it doesn't.*

As for longevity, environmentally-friendly German consumer magazine *Öko Test* found that manufacturers of CFL bulbs fibbed about how long they lasted in order to justify their higher price. 16 of 32 bulbs tested gave up the ghost after 6,000 hours, far less than advertised. And CFLs don't blow like incandescent bulbs; they simply get dimmer as they age.

Dan Norris boasted that the switchover could save a million tonnes of carbon dioxide annually by 2020. The Office for National Statistics says that the UK emitted 707m tonnes of CO_2 equivalent in 2007. While we're sitting in the dark, the Lung-ching coal-fired power station in Taiwan emits 43.3 million tonnes of CO_2 a year.

All this expense and inconvenience to switch to a technology that is about to be superseded. Already being installed in some traffic lights, LED bulbs give out a warm and bright light, are far more adaptable and efficient than CFLs, last far longer, work easily with dimmers and contain nothing toxic. Although expensive, they're still more cost-effective than CFLs and prices are falling. Our bulbs may not be incandescent, but we are.

sex

Sex is used to sell just about everything, from cars to deodorant to chocolate. It helps that the word is short and distinctive, of course, as it can be printed correspondingly larger than a word like, for instance, 'fornication'.

The word itself will appear on the cover of just about every women's magazine, and is guaranteed to sell more copies of newspapers. What's on offer, however, usually falls far short of what has been promised.

A side issue is the promotion of sex aids themselves, which can make outlandish claims safe in the knowledge that any unhappy punter who finds their 'natural viagra' didn't keep them up all night will be far too embarrassed to complain to any trading standards authority – just

as publicans routinely keep condom and similar pub machines empty, safe in the knowledge that few punters are going to complain in person and demand their money back at a crowded bar.

When is a strawberry not a strawberry?

WHEN IT DOESN'T contain any strawberries, is the painful answer. A survey by the Food Commission of 28 supposedly strawberry-flavour drinks and snacks showed that they contained woefully small proportions of real strawberry, and 60 percent of the products tested contained no strawberries whatsoever.

Top of the list came Strawberry Ribena, which was found to have the highest strawberry content of all – but even that was a mere six per cent (compared with nearly eight teaspoons of sugar per serving).

Despite the fact that nearly all the products tested boasted of their 'strawberry flavour' and showed images of glistening, juicy strawberries on the packaging, most of this flavouring was found to be entirely artificial.

Among the worst culprits were:

- Strawberry flavour Angel Delight – contains no strawberries
- Hartley's Strawberry Jelly – contains no strawberries
- Frijj Strawberry Milkshake – contains no strawberries
- Ambrosiá Strawberry Flavour Custard – claims to contain no artificial colours or flavours, no artificial sweeteners, and no preservatives. The label fails to point out that it also contains no strawberries.

A spokesman for the Food Commission described the practice as 'misleading and deceptive. Unfortunately, it's also legal and widespread.' See page 6 for the reason why 'strawberry flavour' is still a legal claim.

small print

Small print is the fine text used to provide loopholes for extravagant claims made in headlines. It often expresses precisely the opposite meaning of the main text, and is always used to mislead or confuse a potential purchaser. It isn't small for reasons of space: it's small to stop us reading it.

● *The lettering for '99p' in this poster is over 2000 times the size of the small print, which begins: 'Price may vary . . . '*

Bargain debasement: the multi-pack scandal

WE'RE SO TRUSTING of our big-name supermarkets that we often fail to notice when they're pulling a fast one. If the label tells us that a multi-pack is better value than buying items individually, we tend to accept the proposal without question.

But, as our research has found, multi-packs often charge a premium for the dubious convenience of bundling several items in a single package.

In Sainsbury's, for instance, we recently found their own-brand orange juice priced at 86p a carton, with a truly money-saving offer of three for £2. Next to these was a four-pack of the same juice, labelled 'Bigger Pack, Better Value'. No price was shown on the four-pack, and it turned out at the till that the 'better value' pack cost £2.91 as opposed to the £2.86 the cartons would have cost if bought separately.

Also in Sainsbury's, we were intrigued by their offer of tuna chunks at 79p a tin compared with the multi-buy pack at £3.25.

Even for those shoppers not armed with a calculator, a glance at the price per 100g is enough to show that the four pack is worse value than buying individual tins – 58.9p for the four pack, 57.2p when bought individually.

'We're doing all we can to reduce pricing errors,' Sainsbury's told us. But three months later, the 'errors' we alerted them to remained unchanged. They did, however, send us a £10 voucher in compensation. Who says complaining isn't worthwhile?

● *Multi-pack bargains: not always the bargain you might expect.*

Olfactory enhancement: we're being led by the nose

THERE WAS A TIME when cleaning products did not smell of pine forests. Then, in 1992, a study found that consumers preferred cleaning stuff to smell of lemon rather than coconut, and suntan oil to smell of coconut instead of lemon. Since then, companies have come to realise the importance of scent in influencing people. A paper by Harvest Consulting says that 'Aromas can help induce consumers to spend money, and many companies are experimenting with the new science of smell to create optimal shopping environments.'

In Germany, a company called DVK – 'System Leader in the Field of Olfactory Enhancement of Indoor Air' – designs 'air vitalizing' systems for retailers, using 'natural hypoallergenic mood olfactory substances which unite the scents diffused by biotopic flora'. *Time* magazine quoted DVK's Diotima von Kempski as saying, 'If people feel good, they spend more. It has to be natural, not artificial. The strongest effect comes when the fragrance is barely discernible.'

In America, fragrance company Demeter specialises in producing quirky but evocative scents such as farm dirt, crayons, jelly beans and soap. But they also provide scents for shops selling clothes and shoes, for car manufacturers, for department stores and many others. Retailers have woken up to the fact that customers can be fooled by smell, even if they're not aware of it.

Airlines often put their own particular scents on their hot towels, and British Airways reportedly infuse the scent of freshly cut grass and salty sea air into their business class lounge at Heathrow Airport.

After complaints that their cars weren't as good as they used to be, Rolls-Royce analysed the smell of the classic 1965 Silver Cloud, reproduced it, and now all their cars smell like that. Without realising that they're being manipulated, their

customers are happier to splash out hundreds of thousands of pounds on a new Roller.

Stores do it. Hotels do it. In the UK, industrial gas group BOC has a division that specialises in creating specific scents derived from 17,000 different fragrances. These are dissolved in liquid carbon dioxide and pumped through the air conditioning system. And it isn't only the ever-popular smell of freshly-baked bread for supermarkets: they once devised a custom mulled-wine smell to put Woolworths' customers into a suitably festive Christmas mood.

Even cinemas tried it in their struggle against television. In 1960, *Scent of Mystery* was released in Smell-O-Vision, a system whereby scents relevant to the story were pumped into the auditorium. Marred by technical problems, it wasn't a success, prompting the comedian Henny Youngman to say: 'I didn't understand the film. I had a cold.'

Perhaps the strangest olfactory addition is that used in the Craven Arms pub in Birmingham. Mindful of the lack of atmosphere since the smoking ban came into force, landlady Sarah Thornton took to spraying the smell of stale cigarettes into the air – which is the scent that makes customers feel like they've had a proper night out, she says.

Too dishonest by half

JUST HOW HONEST are the claims of discounts and special offers made by retailers? Canny customers have long suspected that cries of '15% off', 'Today only' or 'half price' aren't quite what they seem. After all, there's a store in Oxford Street that has had a 'Closing Down' sale for as long as we can remember.

In 2008, a Trading Standards Institute report said that, 'many High Street sales bargains are made to look far more short-term than is really the case so as to make consumers buy without properly comparing prices. Apparent huge discounts, based currently on artificially inflated 28-day prices, drive consumers into making instant purchases in the belief that such huge discounts won't be around very long, or indeed that there cannot in that store be many such bargains, when in fact there is no local or national limit on the number of items that can be sold at that markdown.'

The practice of retailers, particularly supermarkets, increasing the cost of items, just so they can then make massive supposed reductions, was supposed to have been brought to an end by the Consumer Protection from Unfair Trading Regulations Act of 2008. Amongst other things, the legislation outlaws information which, even if it is actually correct, would persuade the average customer to make a transaction that they would not have made otherwise. Towards the end of 2008, however, consumer watchdog *Which?* found that there were still plenty of phony and misleading offers around. Among their findings:

- The law says an item must be at full price for a month before a price is cut, but Waitrose sold blueberries at 'half price' after only two weeks.
- Marks & Spencer sold 'half price' cherries for £2.49 when they'd been priced at £2.99 before.
- Tesco kept strawberries at 'half price' for three months, even though discounts should only last for a month.

It seems to us that there's a good deal of soft fruit that's always on offer at supermarkets at 'half price'. When one customer who thought it must be against the law wrote to her local Trading Standards Office, they actually rang her back to explain. Although

● *Consumers can understand 'half price', it seems, but not more complicated fractions – as this Argos poster shows.*

it's normally forbidden to offer goods at a discount unless they've been on sale at the higher price for a month, in the case of perishable goods, they can be reduced to make sure that the food is not wasted. It's a loophole and so of course the supermarkets exploit it.

The practice of 'marking up to mark down' was supposed to have been curtailed by the new Act, but *Which?* found that, just to give one example, Sainsbury's sold Gallo Chardonnay Sauvignon and Cabernet Zinfandel for £3.99, claiming it was '£1 off' for five weeks, then stuck it back up to £4.99 for a week before making it '£1 off' again. Malcolm Gluck, author of *The Great Wine Swindle*, says that, 'the discounted price is very often the "real price", and has been funded by the wine grower, not the supermarket.'

As for those special offers at the ends of aisles, such as three bottles of wine for £10, you should bear in mind that they might actually have been paid for by the wine producer in order to promote their product, in much the same way that some prominent book displays in bookshops require a sweetener from publishers.

The tourism trap: when all is not as it seems

WE'RE USED TO TALES of woe from holidaymakers who arrive at Spanish hotels only to find they're not yet finished. We've all read about scandals such as the holiday brochure describing a hotel as 'at the seafront', only to change this to 'five minutes' walk from the sea' when inspectors discovered a dual carriageway and a railway line between the hotel and the beach.

But these are petty infractions compared with some of the downright fakery being perpetuated in the name of getting us to part with our holiday cash.

Among the culprits:

- Visit Scotland, the national tourism agency, used Finnish model Katja Halme to be 'the welcoming face of Scotland' in 2002. Four years later, they marketed their winter breaks.

- *Welcome to Alberta, Canada – except this beach happens to be in Northumberland.*

using the face of typical Highland (but sadly Polish) lass Agnes Gornicka.

● In 2007, keen to promote Scottish winter sports, Visit Scotland found itself suffering from a series of unseasonally mild winters. And so they used photographs from the 1990s to show potential visitors the sort of snow-capped delights they could expect.

● Visit Scotland. Again. This time they filmed a promotion for Scotland in autumn, using a girl called Autumn playing with beautiful golden-brown leaves. Except the leaves turned out to be made of plastic. But the girl really was called Autumn, they insisted.

● The Costa Brava, wanting to show the charms of its sandy beaches, used photographs of a Bahamas beach in their promotional material. A month later, they used an image of a beach in Australia.

● A television commercial for Stratford-upon-Avon showed an actor delivering stirring lines from Henry V outside a typical Stratford castle. Except the location used was actually Stokesay Castle, Ludlow, which is over 60 miles away – despite the voiceover proclaiming it to be 'the heart of England, home to Shakespeare's Stratford'.

● A promotional advertisement as part of a £14m rebranding exercise for Alberta, Canada, portrays a boy and girl scampering along an idyllic sandy beach. All very well, except that the beach in question turns out to be Bamburgh in Northumberland, thousands of miles away. A spokesman for the Alberta Public Affairs Bureau commented: 'at one point in the narrative we mentioned our regard for people in other places.' So that's all right then.

The penicillin myth: don't drink and pill-pop

'NO THANKS,' you say, turning down a drink with your mates for the fourth time that evening, 'I can't. I'm on antibiotics.'

It's one of those pervasive pieces of received wisdom, like the fact that swans can break your arm and red sunsets promise a sunny tomorrow. From our mothers' laps onwards, we've been cautioned never to indulge in alcoholic liquor when we're on a course of antibiotics.

The advice is entirely erroneous, and is a myth that has its origins in the Second World War. Soldiers both on leave and abroad were particularly prone to fraternising with whichever local women would entertain them for a consideration, and the incidence of VD (venereal disease) was correspondingly high.

The best way to contain an outbreak was to stop it spreading, by inhibiting further sexual contact until the penicillin had run its course. The problem was that soldiers felt better long before they had fully recovered, and were wont to spread their passion around at the earliest possible opportunity.

Doctors reasoned that alcohol leads to sex, and sex spreads VD, so the best course of action was to tell them not to drink. Merely advising patients to stay off the demon booze wasn't enough, so they invented a mismatch between alcohol and penicillin. Pharmacologically, we're told there's no problem at all with drinking while on most antibiotics.

Just be sure to read the small print first, though.

Buyer (and surfer) beware

RESVERATROL IS A CHEMICAL found in grape skins that, scientists thought, might be linked to long life. Since the discovery in 1993, a number of dietary supplement companies have marketed the extract with extravagant and often ludicrous claims.

The *New York Times* recently ran a scathing article entitled 'With Resveratrol, Buyer Beware', in which it detailed the 'grossly misleading advertising' that accompany marketing of the health additive, singling out TV journalist Barbara Walters who condemns the use of her name to promote it.

Some surprise, therefore, that when the feature appeared on the *New York Times* website, it was accompanied by . . . an advertisement for resveratol, right next to the story, with the line 'as seen on Barbara Walters'. It seemed readers could make up their own minds about the additive, then click to buy it if they didn't agree with the *Times* editorial. After all, who could resist the tempting offer to live to 150?

It's not just downright embarrassing for the publication; the newspaper also profits every time a reader clicks on the ad.

Editing history: what did Obama really say?

WHEN SUSAN WATTS, *Newsnight*'s science editor, presented a piece on Barack Obama's approach to the problem of global warming and other environmental issues, she introduced it with a short film. The images were tasteful shots of a broken-down greenhouse (geddit?) forming the background to an excerpt from the new President's inauguration speech.

This is the speech as it appears in the opening sequence of the film:

> *We will restore science to its rightful place, roll back the spectre of a warming planet. We will harness the sun and the winds and the soil to fuel our cars and run our factories.*

Stirring stuff – and it does, indeed, confirm Obama's green credentials and his determination not to let scientific 'advances' lead to further global warming.

Except this is not what he said. Or, rather, the quote had been edited together from several sections of the speech to give a rather different emphasis.

This is the text from which these excerpts were taken:

> *The state of the economy calls for action, bold and swift, and we will act – not only to create new jobs, but to lay a new foundation for growth. We will build the roads and bridges, the electric grids and digital lines that feed our commerce and bind us together. **We will restore science to its rightful place**, and wield technology's wonders to raise health care's quality and lower its cost. **We will harness the sun and the winds and the soil to fuel our cars and run our factories**. And we will transform our schools and colleges and universities to meet the demands of a new age . . . We will begin to responsibly leave Iraq to its people, and forge*

THE FIRST 100 DAYS:
THE ENVIRONMENT

*a hard-earned peace in Afghanistan. With old friends and former foes, we will work tirelessly to lessen the nuclear threat, and **roll back the spectre of a warming planet.** We will not apologise for our way of life . . .*

When Obama referred to 'restoring science to its rightful place' he used the phrase in the context of health care and the economy. When he talked about 'rolling back the spectre of a warming planet' it was a plea for international cooperation to stem the rise of global warming. Susan Watts then began her report with the words: 'President Obama couldn't have been clearer today. And for most scientists his vote of confidence would not have come a moment too soon.'

To take the quotes out of context, and to rearrange them to give a different meaning, is the sound equivalent of using Photoshop to place people in different settings – a practice the BBC would never condone.

The *Newsnight* editor, Peter Rippon, defended the editing: 'The aim was to give people an impression or montage of what Obama said about science in his inauguration speech. This was signposted to audiences with fades between each point.'

There were no fades in the broadcast version, despite Rippon's claim. It was skilfully edited to sound like one continuous speech. This is not just poor journalism: it's downright unethical.

On the buses

TRY GETTING CHANGE for your bus fare in Bristol and the chances are you won't get coins but a piece of paper instead. First Bus, who operate bus services across the UK, are issuing 'change tickets' instead of money where the driver doesn't have enough change. Cleaner Catherine Jolliffe complained when she was handed one instead of forty pence change, even though the driver's shift had just begun.

She tried using the ticket on another bus but was told it could only be redeemed at one of two First Travel Shops in Bristol, even though the bus journey to get to the closest would have cost more than forty pence. First Bus explained that they had to stop allowing passengers to exchange them on buses as some people were fraudulently copying and using them. Rather more difficult to copy coins of the realm, which would have been Ms Jolliffe's preference for giving change.

First Bus give passengers only 14 days to redeem their tickets in person at a First Travel Shop, or their change is lost for good. As Ms Jolliffe says, it might only have been forty pence but, 'multiply that by the number of people who are using buses and it's a considerable amount that First are pocketing. That money belongs to the customers.'

The next bus has gone

Bristol has buses with no change. In Nuneaton they have a bus shelter with no buses. To the surprise of Warwickshire County Council, they recently discovered that a bus shelter with seats and advertisements had been erected in Eastboro Way in Nuneaton, even though buses have never gone down the street. The shelter was put up ten years ago and has subsequently been regularly cleaned and maintained by J C Decaux, who have a contract from the council, putting up bus shelters for free in exchange for being able to advertise on them. It's never been used, no planning permission for it has ever been found, but it's still there.

A spokesman for the local council said: 'As it stands, the bus shelter provides information, seats, comfort and shelter to pedestrians.' Information? Presumably the information that if they're waiting for a bus, they're going to have a long wait.

Bending the truth

In London, the introduction of the articulated, so-called 'bendy buses' met with a mixed reaction. Transport for London were ticked off for an early advertisement which tried to win over passengers by claiming 'a faster boarding time' than the old, iconic, double-deck Routemasters. But while passengers not fluent in transportation vernacular might assume that 'faster boarding time' meant that the buses wouldn't be at bus stops as long, 'boarding time' actually refers to the time people take to pass through the bus doors. 'Dwell time' is the jargon for the period between the bus stopping and starting again.

The Advertising Standards Authority found that TfL's own study showed that while passengers moved through the doors of the bendy buses more quickly, the 'dwell time' was only quicker if 10 passengers or more boarded. Otherwise Routemasters pipped them.

It was Mayor Ken Livingstone who brought in the bendy buses in 2002 and gradually phased out the Routemaster. This, despite him saying just the previous year that 'only a ghastly dehumanised moron would want to get rid of the Routemaster.'

pro bono

The phrase is short for 'pro bono publico', a Latin term for work done literally 'for the public good', and is used to denote work done for no fee. It's most often used of lawyers working for clients on a low income, at no charge.

A slightly different meaning, then, to that claimed by historian Dr David Starkey, who charged the British Library a fee of £30,000 for curating an exhibition on Henry VIII. When challenged on this figure by the *Sunday Times*, he replied: 'I'd normally charge £50,000 to £100,000 for work of that kind, if I was working for a commercial outfit,' adding: 'I regard it as pro bono work for a public body. It's a public benefit.' Pro bono? Not as we understand it.

life

You might think that a 'life sentence' meant just that or, at the very least, a good many years. Yet in 2006, the Home Office admitted that some of those sentenced to life imprisonment were being released after just 15 months in prison, among them a violent rapist and a man with a penchant for attacking people with hammers.

In 2005, a record 351 'lifers' were freed from prison, almost three times the number in 2000. In 2006, the average time served by a mandatory lifer was 13 years, with 6 years served by other lifers, half the average in 1997.

The cheap bike that could cost you an arm and a leg

WHEN ASDA ANNOUNCED they were going to start selling 'the cheapest bicycle in the UK' – a full-size adult mountain bike for just £70 – they thought they were on to a winner.

Cue red faces all round when they had to pull their TV advertising following a stream of complaints from cyclists. For it seems that the boffins at Asda had taken the self-assembly machine (that's one reason it was so cheap) and, er, self-assembled it incorrectly. With the front forks facing backwards, as they did on the advertisements, the brakes wouldn't work properly and there would be a high risk of serious injury.

Asda themselves tried to make light of the issue, with a tongue-in-cheek press statement: 'As soon as we spotted the error, we put the brakes on the TV ad and pulled it. Our agency is back-pedalling as we speak and we will be wheeling out the new one tomorrow.' Most amusing. And certainly a joke to be enjoyed from the comfort of one's hospital bed.

The true cost of free* flights

RYANAIR, EVERYONE'S LEAST favourite budget airline, is once again offering free* flights. Yes, it's true* – for the total of zero pounds and zero pence*, less discerning travellers can travel from London Stansted to a range of European destinations, from Angoulême to Verona.

At least Ryanair themselves admit on their website that fares 'don't include optional fees and charges', with a handy key that explains just what extras they'll be stiffing you for. A glance at the table shows the following additional fees:

- **Check-in:** £5 to check in online. Except that if you forget or are unable to do so, it's a whopping £40 to check in at the airport. Can you get on the flight without checking in? Of course not. So in what way is this an 'optional' charge?

- **Payment handling fee:** £5 each way. Each way? Surely you only pay for the flight once? The fee is waived only if you pay by Visa Electron, a debit card that's usually only issued to teenagers. Perhaps that's why airlines choose to support it, safe in the knowledge that most of their passengers won't be able to take advantage of this way of saving money. Ryanair even charge £10 when passengers pay with a Ryanair's own Visa card.

- **Priority boarding fee:** £3 each way. You don't have to pay this, of course, if you don't mind being at the back of the queue and ending up stuck in an uncomfortable seat.

- **Infant fee:** £20. Yup. You may travel free, but your baby costs twenty quid.

- **Baggage fees:** £10 for the first bag, £20 if you pay at the airport. £20 each for the next two bags, plus an exorbitant surcharge of £15 per kilo if your baggage is overweight.

- **Flight change fees:** if you want to change your flight it will cost you £35 online, £55 at the airport. If you want to change the name of one of the passengers, it will cost £100 online and £150 at the airport – despite the fact that it costs Ryanair nothing to change a name on a document.

The free flights are only available Tuesday to Thursday, we were told, so we went ahead and tried to book a flight to Milan on Tuesday, returning two days later. We found the 'free' fare was now £8.99 each way – although there was a fare for 79p the previous Sunday.

Well, fair enough, £8.99 is not going to break the bank. Except that this was accompanied by the £5 check-in fee (each way), and a total of £45.94 in taxes and 'fees' (mysteriously listed as 'Insurance/Wheelchair Levy/Aviation Insurance'). Unlike most travel insurance, there seemed no way of removing this one. Plus, right at the end, we're hit with that £10 payment fee.

Checking in a bag brought the total to £103.92, which may not be a lot for a return flight to Milan but is certainly on the expensive side for a *free* flight to Milan. British Airways, by way of contrast, were able to offer a similar return flight for just £110 – on which you would hope to be treated like a person, rather than like cattle.

So sometimes free really does mean free: but you shouldn't bank on it. EU law states: 'The final price paid shall at all times be indicated . . . including the applicable air fare, taxes, charges, surcharges and fees which are unavoidable'; although we've singled out Ryanair here, all budget airlines cheerfully ignore this directive. When we have to pay for such luxuries as checking in and paying for the flights, we know we're being duped.

*not really

The biggest statistic since records began

IN SEPTEMBER 2009, the news broke that people in Britain had repaid more debt than at any time 'since records began'. An impressive statistic: after all, these records must date back to at least the middle ages, right? Wrong. It seems the Bank of England has only been keeping records 'in their current format' since 1993. But the news that we'd repaid more debt than at any time in the last 16 years just doesn't carry the same shock value.

The catch-all phrase is a journalistic trick used to inflate headlines and to give them a greater sense of urgency and newsworthiness. Here are a few more examples:

- PrintWeek reports that the National Association of Paper Merchants has recorded the highest quarterly bad debt 'since records began'. Only later on do they point out that records didn't begin until 2003

- In 2009 we experienced the hottest June 'since records began'. But the weather only began to be recorded in detail in 1914, which rather dampens the sense of a historically hot month

- In Chicago, June 2009 was the wettest 'since records began' – but there, records began only 50 years ago

- China has seen the highest number of deaths from lightning strikes, reported the China Meteorological Administration in 2007. Before millions of Chinese head underground, however, it's worth pointing out that they didn't begin keeping records until 2000, just seven years earlier

- Scottish children have the healthiest teeth 'since records began', says the National Dental Inspection Programme. Their records began in 2003

- Computer hardware spending has fallen to its lowest level 'since records began', reports computing.co.uk – but records began only in 2001

- Hong Kong air pollution in 2009 was the worst 'since records began' – again, records dated back to just 2000

- Britain's beaches were more littered in 2009 than at any time 'since records began', claimed the Marine Conservation Society – that is, at any time since 2004.

Journalism aside, when the phrase is taken up by politicians we know we need to examine the figures more closely.

In 2009, according to the Labour party, Health Secretary Alan Milburn 'joined NHS staff in celebrating waiting times reaching their lowest level since records began.' Unlike the journalists who take care to research their stories, however, Milburn does not state exactly when these records did begin; and, as we've seen from the debt repayment example, it's easy for the statistic-gathering body – in this case, the government – to change the record-keeping methodology at any point, so as to start afresh with a clean sheet.

Sometimes, the phrase is used in a meaningful way: so when we read that road fatalities are now at their lowest since 1926 it's a truly startling figure, given the far smaller number of cars on the road in those days. The difficulty lies in sorting out the true record-breakers from the mass of imposters, as the currency is debased by gross over-use.

today's

We're constantly being sold household cleaning products for 'today's busy lifestyles', or shampoo for 'today's flyaway hair', or detergent for 'today's tough stains'. Really? Are today's stains that much more recalcitrant than those of twenty years ago? Or are they just pulling a fast one?

the occupier

Letters addressed to 'the occupier' are almost always from estate agents. Invariably, they're thrown away unopened. So why don't estate agents take the trouble to find out the name of the person who lives at that address? Surely this would increase the chances of the letter being opened and read?

The truth is that estate agents don't give a monkey's who lives at your house. It's not you they want, it's your address. You think you own your home? You're just passing through. It's a temporary arrangement. You're the dumb cluck who rather inconveniently happens to be occupying the property at the present time.

———— I wish I hadn't said that ————

'My first rule, THE GOLDEN RULE, ensures that over the economic cycle the Government will borrow only to invest, and that current spending will be met from taxation. My second rule is that, as a proportion of national income, public debt will be held at a prudent and stable level over the economic cycle. And to implement these rules, I am announcing today a five year deficit reduction plan.'

Gordon Brown, Budget speech, July 1997. It is forecast that government debt will double to 79% of GDP by 2013, the highest level since World War 2.

Consult and ignore

VOTER APATHY CLEARLY worries politicians. After all, if the voting numbers keep declining, it gets ever harder to claim to be doing something on behalf of 'the people'. So politicians have conjured up various ploys to give the impression of being democratic, one of their favourites being the 'consultation exercise'. What could be more democratic than consulting the opinion of the people who will be affected by whatever policy is being considered?

Unfortunately for poor Joe Public, consultation exercises are only democratic if the Government, or the local authority, or whoever is canvassing opinion, actually listens to what people say. If they don't, it's not just undemocratic, but downright autocratic.

Congestion change

When, in 2004, London Mayor Ken Livingstone proposed extending the Congestion Charge Zone westwards, Transport for London announced a public consultation exercise: 'The ten-week-long consultation will include a leaflet drop to 3.3 million households, 250,000 businesses and 1,400 key stakeholders throughout London asking for their comments.'

Despite this, many residents complained that they didn't know about the consultation, the largest ever carried out by TfL. Only 2% of households responded. Of those who did respond, 77% weren't in favour, 48% being strongly against. 89% of businesses opposed it. Only 6% of people were in favour, most of them apparently already in the existing Congestion Charge zone. 11 petitions opposed it, signed by a total of 28,000 people.

What happened? It went ahead anyway. Ken Livingstone said of the consultation: 'I think it's a complete charade. I think I should make the decisions for London . . . A consultation is not a referendum.'

It's in the post

In 2008-9, over 2,500 Post Offices were closed down in an attempt to stem losses. Although local people were, in theory, consulted, the Public Accounts Committee criticised the speed of the exercise and the way it was handled.

The chairman of the Committee, Edward Leigh, said: 'Given the crucial importance to many in the community of a local post office, I am amazed at the feeble attempts to communicate

with people. The consultation period lasted only a few weeks and research showed that just 18 per cent of people knew they were being consulted . . . I regard the consultation as little more than a sham; the department ran roughshod over local residents' concerns and bulldozed the proposals through.'

Something in the water

In Southampton and south-west Hampshire in 2009, 10,000 people responded to a consultation on whether to add fluoride to their water supply. 78% were against the medication of their water supply, as were the majority of those questioned in a telephone poll. No surprises for guessing that, despite most people not wanting fluoridation, it went ahead anyway.

In the past, water companies had refused appeals by the authorities to fluoridise water, apparently fearing lawsuits. So the 2003 Water Act was enacted, giving local health authorities the power to order fluoridation, and legally indemnifying the water company providing there was advance consultation. Health authorities in many other parts of the UK (though not Scotland) are now planning similar 'consultations' before adding fluoride to their

water supply. If that is democracy, then 'Wij zijn Nederlanders'.

Professor Tony Travers at the London School of Economics thinks there are so many consultations these days because politicians feel unloved. 'Many politicians, particularly at the national level, now feel that the public really doesn't like or trust them and if only they could work out what the public really wanted then the public would come to like politicians once again.'

Just occasionally, of course, a consultation does have an effect. Part of Labour's plans for widening democracy included giving the public the chance to start petitions on the Downing Street website. Peter Roberts started one to oppose Government plans for national road pricing, which notched up over 1.8m signatures – an extraordinary example of democracy in action. Prime Minister Tony Blair sent an email to everyone who signed up saying that he saw it as 'the beginning, not the end of the debate . . . Before we take any decisions there would be further consultations. The public will, of course, have their say, as will Parliament.'

The scheme appears to have been quietly forgotten.

world

We may read of David Beckham as being a 'world class footballer', and that's an understandable claim – he has played for his country and other teams all over the world. But when we see a hotel described as 'world class', what can this possibly mean? That it accepts visitors from overseas? Is there another type of hotel that only serves locals?

'World', like 'universal', is becoming another weasel word that promises much but delivers almost nothing. The problem is not a new one: after all, US baseball competition The World Series has been running unchallenged since 1903, despite the fact that only two countries – the United States and Canada – take part. And since only one Canadian team competes, we suspect they're only there to make the event look less parochial than it really is.

weasel words

When a weasel sucks a bird's egg, it does so surreptitiously, leaving the egg looking untouched. Weasel words are words and phrases that appear to be full of meaning, but which turn out to be as empty as a hollowed-out egg.

Examples include 'studies show that . . . ', 'there is evidence that . . . ', 'people say . . . ' and so on. Which studies? What evidence? Who are these people?

Politicians and advertisers bombard us with weasel words on a daily basis. Drinks are 'enhanced' with nutrients; industries are 'robust' and 'vibrant'. Feel-good words they may be, but the feeling is fleeting.

Autotune that tune!

AS FAR BACK as 1998, Cher released her dance hit 'Believe', which *Billboard* described as, 'the best darn thing Cher has done in years'. Only it wasn't just Cher's powerful voice that booms out of the speakers: it was helped along by a new computer program, Autotune, which corrects singing so that it's always in tune.

Once Autotune has been told what key the song is in, it analyzes the waveform and corrects the pitch to the closest note in that key. With software advances, Autotune is able to perform this feat in real time – which has made it a staple component of gigging musicians, from Shania Twain to 'N Sync.

What it means, of course, is that the sound we hear when we see our favourite acts playing live is not only enhanced by reverb and other echo devices, it's also electronically altered to make them sound better than they really are.

As an unnamed recording engineer told *Time* magazine in 2009: 'Let's just say I've had Autotune save vocals on everything from Britney Spears to Bollywood soundtrack albums. And every singer now presumes that you'll just run their voice through the box.'

Not all singers approve of the technology: Allison Moorer's album *Miss Fortune* carries the sticker 'Absolutely no vocal tuning or pitch-correction was used in the making of this record.'

But as Marco Alpert of Antares Audio Technologies, who make Autotune, puts it: 'If you're a bad singer and sing out of tune, it'll turn you into a bad singer who's now singing in tune.'

Lying for the state

IN 2006, AFTER CRITICISM that troops fighting in Afghanistan lacked the right vehicles and other necessary kit, Tony Blair, then Prime Minister, said that they would be given whatever was needed. 'If the commanders on the ground want more equipment – armoured vehicles for example, more helicopters – that will be provided. Whatever package they want, we will do.'

Yet over the intervening years, soldiers and their families – often bereaved – insisted that there still wasn't enough equipment of the right kind. Various coroners blamed 'notoriously bad' radios, inadequately armoured vehicles and insufficient night vision equipment for the deaths of servicemen and women.

In 2009, the retiring army chief General Sir Richard Dannatt, claimed there was still a lack of helicopters and other kit in Afghanistan. However, Gordon Brown, by then Prime Minister, insisted that the army has 'the resources it needs to be successful' while Armed Forces Minister Bill Rammell said that, 'This is not a government that has starved its military of resources". The incoming army chief, General Sir David Richards, suggested that with the resources they had, the mission in Afghanistan could last 30 or 40 years, a remark that week's Defence Minister, Bob Ainsworth, claimed was 'ludicrous'.

Yet ministers must have known that even if they had the political will and the budget to order more equipment for the troops, the chances of it turning up were very slight, given the staggering ineptitude of the Ministry of Defence. In 2007, a report by MPs found that the Ministry of Defence's biggest weapons projects were £2.6 billion over budget and a total of 36 years behind schedule – six times longer than the Second World War lasted.

It accused ministers of 'massaging' figures by claiming that they had cut the costs of the 20 projects by £781m, when two thirds of that was not a real saving but simply shuffling money from one budget to another.

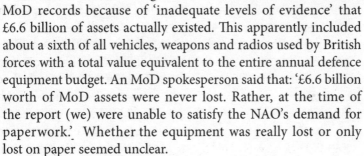

In August 2009, the National Audit Office refused to sign off on MoD records because of 'inadequate levels of evidence' that £6.6 billion of assets actually existed. This apparently included about a sixth of all vehicles, weapons and radios used by British forces with a total value equivalent to the entire annual defence equipment budget. An MoD spokesperson said that: '£6.6 billion worth of MoD assets were never lost. Rather, at the time of the report (we) were unable to satisfy the NAO's demand for paperwork.' Whether the equipment was really lost or only lost on paper seemed unclear.

Even more damning was a report commissioned by Defence Secretary John Hutton. This was due to be published in July 2009 but was suppressed by Hutton's successor, Bob Ainsworth. Written by businessman Bernard Gray, who had been a special adviser to Labour defence ministers, it was leaked to the *Sunday Times* and was still more damning than the earlier report. It claimed that projects were over budget by £35bn, on average five years late and 40% over budget. Lambasting the MoD for utter incompetence, he demanded to know: 'How can it be that it takes 20 years to buy a ship, or aircraft, or tank? Why does it always seem to cost at least twice what was thought? Even worse, at the end of the wait, why does it never quite seem to do what it was supposed to?'

In a blunter manner than is usual in such reports, he went on, 'The problems, and the sums of money involved, have almost lost their power to shock, so endemic is the issue. It seems as though military equipment acquisition is vying in a technological race with the delivery of civilian software systems for the title of "world's most delayed technical solution". Even British trains cannot compete.' He accused politicians of failing to make 'difficult choices' on defence spending, lambasting the government for not having conducted a strategic defence review since 1998 and of expecting limited British forces to do more than they were capable of.

He concluded that these problems 'harm our ability . . . to conduct difficult current operations'. Clearly, though, his 296-page report was misguided, for Armed Forces Minister Bill Rammell insisted that 'Lives are not being put at risk as a result of the procurement process.'

Military press officer John Salisbury-Baker resigned in August 2009, saying he had been forced to tell 'government lies' to the families of dead servicemen as well as to the media, and that it had made him ill. He maintained that he was told to say that soldiers were properly equipped when he knew that was untrue and 'morally indefensible'. The official response? 'It would be inappropriate to comment when proceedings are pending.'

The Chinook fiasco

The chairman of the Commons Public Accounts Committee called the programme for procuring Chinook Mk3 helicopters 'one of the most incompetent procurements of all time.' In 1995, the MoD ordered eight Chinook Mk3s from Boeing for £259 million on behalf of the special forces. They were delivered in 2001. However, despite the armed forces screaming for more helicopters in Afghanistan, eight years later they still hadn't gone into service but have been stored in dehumidified, climate-controlled shelters at Boscombe Down in Wiltshire.

The MoD, it turned out, bought the helicopters but not the source codes for the complicated cockpit avionics software. As it was impossible to see if they passed the regulations on airworthiness, they could only be flown in cloudless skies at a minimum of 500ft. That's not much use to the SAS, or anybody else hoping to have an element of surprise. For years, the MoD and ministers blamed Boeing for refusing to hand over the codes. But it later transpired that the fault lay with the MoD. They had

decided to try to save money by not paying £40m for the Boeing software, thinking that they could invent their own, even though Boeing warned against it. To the surprise of nobody but the dullards at the MoD, it did not work.

In 2004, with troops desperately needing helicopters in Iraq, the MoD negotiated with Boeing for an upgrade to the choppers. The negotiations took 30 months, but the modifications would have cost £215 million and the helicopters wouldn't have been ready until 2011. So the MoD changed their minds again and decided to turn the Chinooks into ordinary troop-carrying helicopters as a cheap way of getting them into service more quickly, although the cost of that rose from an estimated £53 million to almost £100 million.

Just storing and checking the Chinooks for eight years has cost over half a million pounds. At the time of writing, the first test flight had finally gone ahead and it is estimated that they will be in service by some time in 2010. The total cost is likely to be well over £500 million. As for the SAS, the MoD came up with a cunning plan, opting to upgrade some Chinook Mk2s. Only the National Audit Office discovered that the 'night enhancement package' on these and other Chinooks actually impaired the pilots' visibility and it is thought they were a contributing factor in two crashes.

According to *The Guardian*, 87,000 people work at the MoD, more than the personnel of the RAF and Navy combined. 23,000 of them are in the procurement agency – three times the number needed during the Second World War.

In July 2009, even before two Chinooks had to be destroyed to stop the Taliban getting them, the Commons Defence Select Committee said a lack of helicopters was undermining UK forces in Afghanistan. But those eight Chinooks are still in their hangars at Boscombe Down.

vanilla

Good ice cream is flavoured with vanilla. But if it's only vanilla flavour, the chances are the taste will come from Vanillin instead. 'Vanillin' may sound just like vanilla, but it's the trade name given to the compound 4-hydroxy-3-methoxybenzaldehyde ($C_3H_8O_3$) that's very much cheaper to manufacture.

Vanillin is made, in part, through the fermentation of Lignin, a constituent of wood and a waste by-product of the paper industry. Yum yum!

aqua

The magic additive that's so powerful it tops the list of ingredients in every shampoo, bubble bath, conditioner, washing liquid and beauty product on the market.

Sounds an awful lot more impressive than plain 'water', doesn't it?

I wish I hadn't said that

'There's nothing going on between us.'

Bill Clinton to his top aides about Monica Lewinsky. Testifying to a Grand Jury about why the above was not a lie, he added: 'It depends on what the meaning of the word "is" is. If the – if he – if "is" means is and never has been, that is not – that is one thing. If it means there is none, that was a completely true statement . . . Now, if someone had asked me on that day, are you having any kind of sexual relations with Ms Lewinsky, that is, asked me a question in the present tense, I would have said no. And it would have been completely true.'

Hillary, meet Hillary

ON A GOODWILL MISSION in Asia in 1995, Hillary Clinton happened to meet – apparently coincidentally – Sir Edmund Hillary. She told the man who, in 1953, was the first to reach the summit of Mount Everest, that her mother had named her after him.

There was some scepticism that Clinton's mother would actually have heard of Edmund Hillary in 1947, given that the New Zealand mountaineer was barely known outside his own country. However, although Clinton had never mentioned the story before and had omitted it from her own autobiography, from now on she insisted that her mother, Dorothy Rodham, had read about him in a magazine. The story became part of her biographical material that her aides handed out and was repeated in Bill Clinton's autobiography *My Life* in 2004.

Then, in October 2006, almost 10 years later, she suddenly admitted that it wasn't true after all. Her spokeswoman Jennifer Hanley revealed that 'it was a sweet family story her mother shared to inspire greatness in her daughter, to great results I might add'. Did she wait until her daughter was almost 60 before she told her the truth? It seems odd, yet the retraction was issued just a week after Hillary's mum moved in with her and Bill in Washington.

e

Not e-numbers, but the precisely typographically-defined lower case letter 'e' that has appeared on packaging since 1974, when it was introduced by the snappily-named 'European Council directive 75/106/EEC of 1974-12-19'.

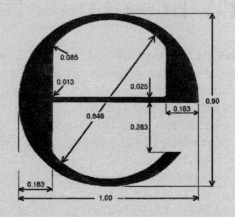

Before that date, the volumes listed on packaging contents – from boxes of matches to baked beans – were a minimum value. So if a box of matches said it contained 45 matches, then you could be sure it contained *at least* 45 matches. In practice, each package was sure to contain more than the number quoted, in order to satisfy the stringent labelling rules while accommodating the vagaries caused by uncertain packaging technology.

Now, however, products can contain up to 9% less than the quantity or amount stipulated on the packaging, as long as the devilish 'e' is present. Buy 100 and you can get just 91. The result: we're now getting less than we pay for, whereas previously we got more.

Cloudy with a chance of meatballs

IN FEBRUARY 1997 Tony Blair told *The Sun* that when he visits his constituency in Sedgefield, 'we often pop down to the local chippie and get a fish and chip supper, my favourite, which we'll eat in front of the TV.' Indeed, a Sedgefield Labour Party election leaflet had also given fish and chips as his preferred dish.

Yet when, in 1998, the NSPCC asked the Prime Minister to contribute the recipe for his favourite meal to the *Islington Cookbook*, he claimed that it was 'fresh fettuccini garnished with a sauce of olive oil, sun-dried tomatoes and capers.'

Journalist Anne Applebaum, writing in the *Sunday Telegraph* in 2001, says that during the 1997 General Election campaign, Blair told journalists that his favourite food was steak and chips.

He must have a lot of favourites. In 1998, when a school in Launceston in Cornwall put together a book of celebrities' favourite recipes, the recipe that came back on Downing Street notepaper was for meatballs in tomato sauce. It was this recipe that also appeared in 1999 in *Parliamentary Portions: Gourmet Recipes from New MPs*.

When interviewed on Blue Peter by Konnie Huq in 2007, he responded to her teasing about his cooking ability by saying, 'I can do more than beans on toast thank you very much. I can do spaghetti bolognese.' Odd that he didn't mention the meatballs, given that his recipe for them is more complicated than spag bol.

Perhaps, as critics claim, Blair was simply saying what he expected each audience wanted to hear. Or maybe he was just a man of ever-changing tastes.

Lies, damned lies
...and statistics

WHEN GORDON BROWN became Prime Minister he promised there would be 'no more spin'. To this end, in 2007 he appointed the deliciously-named Sir Michael Scholar as the first chairman of the new Office for National Statistics. A man who clearly loves his job, he told a journalist: 'Good statistics are as important as sound money or clean water.' He pointed out in another interview that: 'A number of surveys were done which showed that only one in six thought that British official statistics were not manipulated by politicians. The level of trust was very low.'

But the ONS was given control over only a fifth of Government statistics. Those for health, schools, crime and immigration come from the NHS and the relevant ministries. And while Sir Michael and a Commons select committee argued that ministers should only see statistics a few hours before they are issued (French ministers get an hour, the American president just 30 minutes),

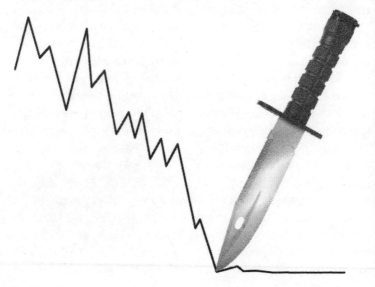

the Government insisted on 24 hours. Why so long, if it isn't to work out how to spin the statistics?

Asked to give an example of the egregious use of statistics, Sir Michael no doubt warmed the cockles of Gordon Brown's heart by referring to the recession in the early 1980s. 'The numbers unemployed in Britain rose every month . . . The government changed the definition of unemployment 23 times in as many months. And every time they changed the definition, the redefinition reduced the number.'

Gordon Brown may not have been as happy with Sir Michael before his first year in the job was up. In December 2008, after a private briefing, the BBC reported the success of the Government's 'Tackling Knives Action Programme'. The Home Secretary Jacqui Smith boasted of a sharp reduction in stabbings: 'The tough, targeted action we are taking in 10 areas is making a real difference on the ground.'

Then it transpired that Home Office statisticians had advised against such an early version of figures being published, but were overruled by a special adviser at No 10, scenting the chance of some decent publicity.

Sir Michael wrote to 10 Downing Street: 'These statistics were not due for publication for some time, and had not therefore been through the regular process of checking and quality assurance. The statisticians who produced them, together with the national statistician, tried unsuccessfully to prevent their premature, irregular and selective release. I hope you will agree that the publication of prematurely released and unchecked statistics is corrosive of public trust in official statistics, and incompatible with the high standards which we are all seeking to establish.'

No wonder, then, that in April 2009 Home Office adviser and former Respect Tsar Louise Casey said that public confidence in crime statistics was so low that the public are no longer surprised if they turn out to be false. Indeed, in July 2009, when the statistics were published, it was clear that the £3m TKAP campaign had not been a particular success. Although ministers spun various numbers, teenagers killed by knives remained unchanged while those killed over the age of 20 went up.

Mind the gap

'Women are paid on average 23 per cent less per hour than men.' So said the outraged Government Equalities Office, in a press release in April 2009 which got plenty of publicity for Equality Minister Harriet Harman's new Equalities Bill.

However, Dame Karen Dunning, the ONS's National Statistician, had complained to the GEO the previous November that their way of calculating gender pay differences was confusing and potentially damaging. They were not, she pointed out, comparing like for like. Instead, they set men's full-time pay against women's part-time pay. For full-time pay, the true gap was 12.8% while, comparing part-time pay, women were actually paid 3.4% more than men. As part-timers get less than full-time workers and there are four times as many women part-timers as men, the GEO's way of presenting the statistics exaggerated the gender pay gap.

There are apparently no statisticians working in the GEO, so you might have thought that they would pay attention to the National Statistician warning them about abusing statistics, particularly given the earlier row over the knife crime figures.

Not a bit of it. After they published the 23% figure, Sir Michael Scholar wrote to Harriet Harman saying that the use of the statistic 'may undermine public trust in official statistics' and 'risks giving a misleading quantification of the gender pay gap'.

While Jacqui Smith had to apologise to the House of Commons over the knife crime statistics, there was no apology from Harman. On the contrary, the GEO clearly thought they understood statistics better than Sir Michael and the ONS

because they told a BBC journalist, 'We believe this figure gives the fullest picture of the country's gender pay gap.'

Just a month later, the Women and Work Commission, a quango based at the GEO, published the number again in a report carried on the department's website. In the foreword, Commission chair Baroness Prosser said, 'Women are still paid, on average, 22.6 per cent less per hour than men.' Not only that, but she went on to claim that 'Pay gaps are even greater for part-time workers (39.9 per cent).'

The aggrieved Sir Michael wrote to Baroness Prosser in August 2009: the figure of '39.9 per cent appears to be a measure of the difference between the median hourly earnings of part-time women compared with full-time men ... Such a comparison needs particularly careful presentation and justification if it is not to mislead ... The casual reader would be surprised to learn then that median hourly earnings of women and of men (excluding overtime) are very close, with women's median pay actually being slightly higher than men's (by 3.4 per cent).'

No apology was forthcoming on this occasion either. Perhaps, unlike Jacqui Smith, Harriet Harman and her department realise that Sir Michael and the ONS have no punitive powers and that the public will probably remember the sizzle of the phony figures rather than the rap on the knuckles.

Fight for a ticket: the great review scam

WHEN IT COMES to dreadful plays and films, it is debatable whether more creativity goes into the production or the mangling of critics' words for the posters. 'A fantastic load of tosh', for instance, might end up on a poster as 'Fantastic'.

- The film *Live Free or Die Hard* carried the blurb 'hysterically . . . entertaining', though the original review said 'hysterically overproduced and surprisingly entertaining.'

- Dominic Maxwell reviewed the stage version of *Saturday Night Fever* in *The Times*. His conclusion that 'If it's an all-out retro-romp you want, this only fitfully delivers' was truncated to: 'An all-out retro-romp!'

- A review of the musical *Zipp!* read: 'If schoolboy innuendo is your bag, book now.' Outside the theatre, potential theatregoers could read that the *Independent on Sunday* had said: 'Book now'.

- Even the National Theatre isn't above such sharp practices. Reviewing *Landscape with Weapon*, the *Daily Telegraph* said: 'If anyone was going to produce a scorching, blinding, lacerating play about the arms industry, I'd have put smart money on that someone being Joe Penhall'. The review made it clear that the play was anything but those things, yet the publicity quote was 'A scorching, blinding, lacerating play about the arms industry.'

In 2008, such creative practices were outlawed in Europe as part of the Unfair Commercial Practices Directive. A misleading quotation that persuades someone to see a film or play could land a producer in hot water, though we aren't aware that this has happened yet. However, in October 2008, Disney were attacked

over their promotion of *The Boy In The Striped Pyjamas* because the 'critics' were not national newspaper or TV reviewers, but Joe Public. 'Simply stunning' and 'please please see this film' said the likes of Theedge-4 and Mjavfc1 when they posted their comments on imdb.com, the Internet Movie Database. As Jason Solomons, chairman of The Critics' Circle film section, pointed out: 'Anybody can make up an internet name – it could be the producer himself or one of the actors.'

With professional critics banned from previews of *The Year of Magical Thinking* on Broadway, producer Scott Rudin was furious when the *New York Times* encouraged readers who had seenm the show to write a review on their website. Retaliating, he used online reviews such as 'An evening of magical theater. Get yourself a ticket' in the ads, quoting 'The New York Times Online.' A deliciously catty – and leaked – correspondence ensued, with Rudin concluding: 'When the Times stops running

Readers' Reviews on its Web site, I'll stop using them in advertising. You can look forward to seeing them anywhere and everywhere until then. If the paper desires to engage with me in a First Amendment dispute, be my guest.'

You know those 'man in the street' TV ads where ordinary punters extol the virtue of movies? Both Columbia and Fox Searchlight admitted that they sometimes got employees to impersonate moviegoers and say complimentary things about their employers' latest movie.

Big name reviews

Perhaps the most gloriously misleading ad campaign was the brainchild of theatrical producer David Merrick, a man who delighted in publicity stunts. He knew he had a turkey on his hands in 1961 with the musical *Subways Are Sleeping*. Yet the poster carried seven quotes such as 'A fabulous musical. I love it' and 'One of the few great musical comedies of the last thirty years', accompanied by the names of New York's top seven theatre critics.

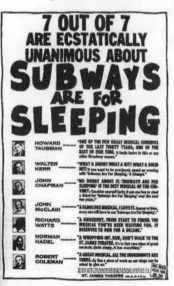

● *Top critics said… or at least, their alter egos did.*

They hadn't written the quotes, though. Instead, Merrick found seven people with the same names, took them to the show, wined them and dined them and asked them what they thought of it. The ad, headed '7 Out Of 7 are ecstatically unanimous about *Subways Are For Sleeping*' was booked for all the main papers, but Merrick overcooked it by carrying photographs of the 'reviewers'. A copy editor realised that the real Richard Watts wasn't black and blew the whistle.

Unfortunately for the *Herald Tribune*, they'd already gone to press. Although it only ran in one edition, the publicity for the stunt was so great that the show ran for nearly six months.

Over Manning

Occasionally, a line is crossed. In 2001, several Sony films which hadn't gone down too well with most critics, even the usual blurb whores, were nonetheless praised to the skies by David Manning of *The Ridgefield Press*. He waxed lyrical over films such as *The Animal*, *The Patriot*, *Vertical Limit* and *Hollow Man*. Perhaps the staff of *The Ridgefield Press* in Connecticut don't go to the movies often because they didn't notice anything untoward. It was only when a *Newsweek* journalist contacted them to ask who David Manning was that they realised they were being quoted. They were somewhat surprised, because they had never heard of David Manning.

That was hardly surprising. Manning was the invention of a Sony senior vice-president of creative advertising, and the director of creative advertising. Creative is right. They'd named him after one of their mates. Presumably bored of having to ask real critics for quotes, they found the fictitious Manning far easier to deal with as he came up with quotes like 'Another winner' and 'One helluva scary ride'. When the news got out, a Sony spokeswoman said: 'It was an incredibly foolish decision and we're horrified.' Presumably she was even more horrified when a judge ordered Sony to pay $1.5m to fans who saw the films Manning puffed.

Although Manning had dubious taste, he was certainly right when, reviewing *A Knight's Tale*, he called Heath Ledger 'This year's hottest new star'. Joe Roth was the boss of Revolution Studios, which made *The Animal*, one of the films Manning extolled. He grumbled: 'If he doesn't exist, he should at least have given us a better quote.'

Beware the humble asterisk, the sphincter of punctuation. Tiny it may be, but it conceals a torrent of effluent and ordure designed purely to cheat you.

Asterisks always travel in pairs and have a typographical quirk: they appear at a tiny size, regardless of the size of the text to which they're attached. Asterisks follow tempting come-on words like Free, New, Half Price and Special Offer. They are the equivalent of the advertiser holding up a sign saying, 'This is a lie'. For every asterisk has its twin, accompanied by a barrage of small print. No point actually reading the diminutive text. Whatever it says, it's legalese for, 'You've been conned.'

The dagger is a typographic device used after an advertiser has exhausted the supply of asterisks and double asterisks. It means the same thing – that there's a lie waiting to be explained in the small print. Really, though, the dagger is just another way of sticking the knife in.

—— I wish I hadn't said that ——

'The House of Lords must go – not be reformed, not be replaced, not be reborn in some nominated life-after-death patronage paradise, just closed down, abolished, finished.'

Neil Kinnock in Tribune, November 1976. Or, as he is now known, Lord Kinnock of Bedwellty. His wife Glenys is now Baroness Kinnock of Holyhead.

The fakes that fooled the museums

ONE OF THE PRIZED EXHIBITS at Amsterdam's Rijksmuseum was a piece of moon rock given to former Dutch Prime Minister Willem Drees by the American ambassador during a world tour by the Apollo 11 astronauts Neil Armstrong, Michael Collins and Buzz Aldrin in 1969. Donated to the museum after Drees's death, it was seen by tens of thousands of visitors every year, marvelling at the rock that had been brought back from another word.

Except it hadn't. To the museum's considerable embarrassment – and the glee of those conspiracy nuts who think we never went to the moon – in 2009 the museum admitted that the 'moon rock' was actually a lump of petrified wood. Nobody seemed sure if the item was the same thing that had been given to Drees. While NASA did donate moon rocks

● *Not a piece of moon rock either*

to over 100 countries, they mostly came from later missions, whereas this was apparently given just a few months after Apollo 11 returned to earth.

Museum spokeswoman Xandra van Gelder said that, 'Apparently no one thought to doubt it, since it came from the Prime Minister's collection.' The museum intends keeping the rock, though, as a curiosity.

In 2003, Southend Museum hurriedly abandoned plans to exhibit a four-foot-long tusk of a woolly mammoth. Dug up in pensioner Dudley Green's back garden, the excitement of

Spot the difference: tusk (top), Victorian clay pipe (bottom)

museum staff faded when it was discovered to be not a 20,000 year-old mammoth tusk, but a Victorian clay water pipe.

The provenance of paintings can be particularly tricky. In 1971, the world's richest man, J. Paul Getty, paid around $1m for a small Rubens study of a black man's head. Intended for his new museum, he was proud that, per square inch, it was the world's most expensive painting. Then it turned out it wasn't by Rubens. The museum claimed for a while that it was by van Dyck, then gave up even on that. It was never shown until, in July 2009, it turned up in the museum's 'sketching gallery', a copy that visitors themselves could copy.

Even exalted museums can make mistakes. In 2008, Madrid's Prado museum mounted *Goya – In Times of War*, an exhibition of work by the leading Spanish artist. Eyebrows were raised when one of Goya's masterpieces, *El Coloso*, a portrayal of the horrors of war, was not included. Renovation had revealed the initials 'AJ', possibly one of Goya's students, in the bottom left of the picture and the museum realised it probably wasn't by the master after all.

Despite never selling any paintings in his lifetime – or perhaps because of it – Van Gogh is apparently the world's most often-forged artist. Van Gogh scandals date back as far as 1928. In 1996,

Van Gogh expert Jan Hulsker remarked of the artist's period in Auvers-sur-Oise that 'the number of paintings attributed to Van Gogh (76) far exceeds the amount of work he could have done in the seventy days he stayed there.'

The following year, the *Art Newspaper* shocked the art world by claiming that up to 45 Van Goghs in public collections such as the Metropolitan Museum, the Musée d'Orsay and even the Van Gogh Museum could still be fakes. A year later 18 of them had been reclassified as fakes or of doubtful authenticity.

The most enjoyable Van Gogh fake, though, cropped up in 1935 when New York's Museum of Modern Art held an exhibition of the artist's work. Veteran prankster Hugh Troy, an artist himself, infuriated by the crowds, was convinced they were ghouls drawn by stories of the artist's tortured life rather than true art connoisseurs.

He sculpted an ear from corned beef and placed it on a table with a sign reading: 'This is the ear which Vincent Van Gogh cut off and sent to his mistress, a French prostitute, Dec. 24, 1888.' To his intense satisfaction, the crowds clustered around the ear, enabling him to examine Van Gogh's paintings in comfort.

● *Goya's El Coloso – but it isn't by Goya after all.*

The height of ambition

NICOLAS SARKOZY, the French President, is 5 feet 5 inches tall. But clearly he doesn't want people to know he is. Since marrying him, Carla Bruni, 5 feet 9 inches, has taken to wearing flat pumps or shoes with low heels while he wears stacked shoes that add two inches to his height. However, Sarkozy, one inch shorter than Napoleon Bonaparte was, still goes to great lengths to look taller than he is.

In April 2009, he was mocked for standing on tiptoes when he was photographed with his wife and the Obamas in Strasbourg (Barack being 6ft 2ins and Michelle 5ft 11ins). Then, in June, a press photographer who was off to one side of Sarkozy as he gave

● *Sarkozy, Obama, Stallone: all the same height, it would seem.*

a speech during the D-Day anniversary ceremonies, got a shot showing that Sarkozy was standing on a low box.

But the laughter could almost be heard across the Channel when Sarkozy visited the Faurecia car parts factory in Normandy in September 2009. A worker interviewed on Belgian TV claimed that she was hand-picked to stand on the podium behind the President specifically because she was short. RTBF TV said that a group of 20 specially-chosen vertically-challenged workers, who didn't work in the unit where Sarkozy was photographed, were bussed in from other areas to make the President look taller. The report, an instant web hit in France, was dismissed as 'absurd and grotesque' by the Elysée. A CFDT union leader, however, claimed that the order to find short workers for the photoshoot had come straight from the Elysée.

In the golden age of Hollywood, the studios went to great lengths to disguise the heights of their more diminutive leading actors. Humphrey Bogart, who was 5ft 8ins, wore blocks on his shoes when playing against Ingrid Bergman in *Casablanca*. Platforms and other devices were constructed so that Alan Ladd, probably the same height as Sarkozy, looked the right height for his leading ladies; poor Sophia Loren had to act in a trench when she was on screen with him.

It's still done today. Macho man Sylvester Stallone is only 5ft 7ins tall, but you wouldn't know it from his movies. When Nicole Kidman and Tom Cruise divorced, she said, 'At least I can wear high heels now.'

bogof

A rather ugly acronym for 'Buy one get one free', a supermarket selling technique that has the distinct advantage that, unlike items labelled as being in a 'sale', there doesn't have to have been a previous time at which one single item was sold at the same price as the two currently on offer.

So it's a bargain, right? We're getting these two items both for half price. Except that in order to get the discount we're having to buy twice as many of them as we want.

Sometimes, the concept is downright idiotic – such as in this advertisement for motorized salt and pepper pots. They're obviously sold as a matching pair: to claim we're only buying one and getting the other at no cost is an insult to our intelligence. They might as well print the same slogan on a pair of shoes.

● *Matching set? No, you only pay for the salt mill . . .*

Buy One, Get One FREE..

Our New stainless steel Salt & Peppers Mills are both stylish and practical. Operated by a simple touch of a button, for use with one hand. Fitted with adjustable grinders so you can select from fine to coarse as suits. The Mills are also fitted with an integrated light in the base to illuminate your plate to show how much has been dispensed. Measures 23cm x 5cm dia (9" x 2"). And uses 4 x AA batteries (not supplied, for batteries see page 98). Buy the Salt Mill and we will send you a FREE Pepper Mill.

24457 Salt Mill with FREE Pepper Mill   £14.95

NEW

In the public eye – and under scrutiny

YOU MIGHT HAVE THOUGHT that people in the public eye would ultra-careful about letting slip too many porkies. We don't mean actresses shaving a year or two off their age, as Amanda Redman was discovered to have done in August 2009, but whoppers so enormous that they're almost certain to be found out.

Take Gordon Ramsay. Being one of the most famous chefs in the world, wasn't it foolish to fib about playing first-team football for Glasgow Rangers? He boasted of it in many interviews, in his autobiography and on 'Desert Islands Discs' in 2002. 'I was with the first team squad,' he told Sue Lawley. 'I played three first team games.' He claimed that, after an injury, he was sacked by manager Jock Wallace and coach Archie Knox.

In fact, as became clear in March 2009, he was only an unsigned tryout. As Knox said when quizzed by journalists, 'He must be a very confused individual. I was the manager of Dundee at the time.'

An unqualified success

Another TV personality, 'Doctor' Gillian McKeith, turned out not to be the sort of doctor most people imagined. Her PhD in 'holistic nutrition' was gained through distance learning from the American Holistic College of Nutrition. Her PhD thesis, however, has never been published. In 2007, after a complaint to the Advertising Standards Authority, McKeith agreed to stop using the title 'Doctor' in advertising and mailshots.

According to *The Guardian*, 'It is understood the ASA was minded to rule that the adverts were misleading, because the college was not accredited by any recognised educational authority at the time she took the course, and she does not hold a general medical qualification. While the adverts usually stated somewhere in the text Ms McKeith was not a medical doctor, the initial impression given was that she was.' Her website now says 'Gillian is not a medical doctor'.

She used to list that she was a 'certified professional' member of the American Association of Nutritional Consultants. That was until Ben Goldacre wrote in *The Guardian*'s 'Bad Science' column that, requiring nothing more than a payment of $60, his dead cat Hettie had also become a 'certified professional' member of the American Association of Nutritional Consultants.

Publicity to the Max

Many celebrities, including Gordon Ramsay, are represented by PR maven Max Clifford. His own website biography ends with news of his second job after starting as a junior sports reporter on the *Merton and Morden News*. 'Next stop was the EMI records press office in 1962, where practically his first assignment was to promote an unknown band from Liverpool called The Beatles. The rest is history . . . '. Hunter Davies, the Beatles' official

● *The star of Glasgow Rangers: in your dreams, Gordon.*

biographer, told *The Guardian*: 'I have about 500 Beatles books, plus about 2,000 magazines, programmes and articles about the Beatles, yet I have not read one reference in them to Mr Clifford's contribution.' He reckons Clifford probably worked on handouts for all EMI's acts in 1962 and 63. 'The real publicity work on the Beatles was done by Epstein himself, who, from as early as 1961, had a full-time publicist working on The Beatles.'

Archer's porkies

When it comes to embroidering a celebrity CV, Jeffrey Archer is in a class of his own. Among assorted untrue claims were:

- his grandfather was the Mayor of Bristol
- he was a fellow of the International Federation of Physical Culture, actually a body-building correspondence course
- he was an undergraduate at Brasenose College in Oxford with six O-levels and three A-levels behind him when he had only 3 O's and took a Diploma in Education at the Oxford Department of Education as a mature student.
- he the youngest MP in Parliament in 1969
- he was the youngest-ever GLC councillor.

A good sportsman, Archer did represent Brasenose and Oxford, but was never the undergraduate he claimed to be. Although he may not have clarified that he went to the minor Wellington School rather than the more prestigious Wellington College, he did nothing to stop others making the assumption.

His wife Mary Archer once admitted to a *Sunday Times* journalist that her husband had 'a gift for inaccurate precis'. His own website still says that he was educated at Brasenose College but at least there is a touch of self-deprecation. While boasting that he once ran 100 yards in 9.6 seconds for Great Britain, he also admits to running the London Marathon in 2004 in 5 hours 26 mins. 'He was overtaken by a camel, a phone-box and a girl walking. He has no plans to repeat the experience.'

Don't quote me...

 'There is a young madman proposing to light the streets of London – with what do you suppose – with smoke!'
Sir Walter Scott on gas lighting

'What can be more palpably absurd than the prospect held out of locomotives travelling twice as fast as stagecoaches?'
The Quarterly Review, 1825

'Rail travel at high speed is not possible because passengers, unable to breathe, would die of asphyxia.'
Dr Dionysus Lardner, Professor of Natural Philosophy and Astronomy, early 19th century

'[When] the Paris Exhibition closes electric light will close with it and no more be heard of.' *Erasmus Wilson, Professor, Oxford University, 1878*

 'The phonograph . . . has no commercial value.'
Thomas Edison

'This "telephone" has too many shortcomings to be seriously considered as a practical form of communication. The device is inherently of no value to us.'
Internal memo, Western Union, 1878

'It will make war impossible.'
Hudson Maxim, inventor of the machine gun, 1893

'Radio has no future. Heavier-than-air flying machines are impossible. X-rays will prove to be a hoax.'
Lord Kelvin, scientist, 1899

'Man will not fly for 50 years.' *Wilbur Wright to brother Orville, 1903*

'That the automobile has practically reached the limit of its development is suggested by the fact that during the past year no improvements of a radical nature have been introduced.'
Scientific American 1909

'Airplanes are interesting toys but of no military value.' *Marshal Foch, Professor of Strategy, Ecole Superieure de Guerre, 1911*

'The energy produced by the breaking down of the atom is a very poor kind of thing. Anyone who expects a source of power from the transformation of these atoms is talking moonshine.'
Ernest Rutherford, shortly after splitting the atom in 1917

'Professor Goddard does not know the relation between action and reaction and the need to have something better than a vacuum against which to react. He seems to lack the basic knowledge ladled out daily in high schools.'
New York times on rockets, 1921

…on science

'To place a man in a multi-stage rocket and project him into the controlling gravitational field of the moon where the passengers can make scientific observations, perhaps land alive, and then return to earth – all that constitutes a wild dream worthy of Jules Verne. I am bold enough to say that such a man-made voyage will never occur regardless of all future advances.' *Lee DeForest, radio scientist and inventor of the vacuum tube, 1926*

'Who the hell wants to hear actors talk?'
Harry Warner, head of Warner Brothers, 1927

'Stocks have reached what looks like a permanently high plateau.'
Irving Fisher, Economics Professor, Yale University, 1929, the year of the Wall Street Crash

'There is not the slightest indication that nuclear energy will ever be obtainable. It would mean that the atom would have to be shattered at will.' *Albert Einstein, 1932*

'The bomb will never go off. I speak as an expert in explosives.'
Admiral William Leahy, about the atomic bomb, 1943

'Television won't be able to hold on to any market it captures after the first six months. People will soon get tired of staring at a plywood box every night.'
Darryl F. Zanuck, head of 20th Century-Fox, 1946

'Computers in the future may weigh no more than 1.5 tons.'
Popular Mechanics, 1949

'Space travel is bunk.'
Sir Harold Spencer Jones, UK Astronomer Royal, 1957, two weeks before Sputnik orbited the Earth

'There is no reason for any individual to have a computer in their home.' *Ken Olsen, founder of Digital Equipment, 1977*

'That virus is a pussycat.' *Dr Peter Duesberg, molecular-biology professor at Berkeley, on HIV, 1988*

Sadly, the following appear not to be true, even though widely quoted:

'Everything that can be invented has been invented.' *Charles H Duell, Comissioner, US Patent Office, 1899*

'I think there is a world market for maybe five computers.' *Thomas J Watson, IBM chairman, 1943*

'640K ought to be enough for anybody.'
Bill Gates, chairman, Microsoft

Don't get fresh with me

IN GORDON RAMSAY'S autobiography, *Humble Pie*, the celebrity chef says: 'Little Chef don't employ chefs – they employ people who can use the technology they have installed to heat up pre-prepared food.'

Somewhat embarrassing, then, when it turned out that 'freshly prepared' food such as fishcakes, coq au vin and braised pig cheeks was actually made in the kitchens of GR Logistics in Wandsworth and then sent by van to one of Ramsay's restaurants and three of his gastropubs to be heated up. The head chef told a reporter from *The Sun* that, 'All you have to do is pop it in a pan of boiling water and reheat it.'

The company admitted it, but insisted the food was still 'freshly prepared'. 'Gordon Ramsay chefs prepare components of dishes devised and produced to the highest Gordon Ramsay standards. These are supplied to those kitchens with limited cooking space such as Foxtrot Oscar and Gordon Ramsay's highly-acclaimed pubs ... These are sealed and transported daily in refrigerated vans and all menu dishes are then cooked in the individual kitchens.'

Only days before, in an interview with the BBC's Olive magazine, Ramsay had said, 'My food hell is any ready meal. It's so easy to prepare a quick meal using fresh produce, such as a simple stir-fry, but people still resort to ready meals that all taste exactly the same.'

The killing foods

Rival chef Antony Worrall Thompson ended up with egg all over his face when, in a magazine interview in 2008, he waxed lyrical about organic foods.

'We have a lot of things growing near the restaurants,' he said. 'We use a lot of nettles at this time of year, mainly for soup. The weed henbane is great in salads.'

Henbane? The same henbane that is a close relative to deadly nightshade? The same henbane that can cause convulsions, hallucinations, vomiting and death? The same henbane Dr Crippen used to poison his wife? The same henbane that Claudius used to murder Hamlet's father? That henbane?

Andrew Chevalier, a fellow of the National Institute of Medical Herbalists, said: 'A good portion would probably cause significant gastrointestinal difficulties and a larger dose would be fatal. If anyone has followed Mr Worrall Thompson's advice they should dial 999 and prepare to have their stomach pumped.'

The next issue of the magazine *Health And Organic Living* had a letter from the editor: 'In our August issue Antony Worrall Thompson suggested that the weed henbane was great in salads – in fact henbane (Hyoscyamus niger) is very toxic and is a Schedule III poison under the Medicines Act. Please discount this suggestion – Antony is very sorry for causing confusion, and had quite a different plant in mind.'

He was apparently thinking of fat hen.

everything

When Debenhams sent out letters to their customers proclaiming '15%* Off Everything All Weekend', they were being less than entirely truthful. Because 'everything' didn't actually mean 'everything' in the sense that you and I might understand it. The asterisk in the headline was the giveaway, for those who chose to look at the small print. The promotion did not, for instance, include cosmetics, wine, kettles, toasters, blenders, mobile phones or many other items.

In this instance, the Advertising Standards Authority ruled that the advert was misleading. But by then, of course, the weekend had long since gone.

special offer

A 'special offer' used to be just that: an offer of goods or services that was unusual or out of the ordinary. Now, all it means is 'for sale'. Some websites have banner advertising slots that have the words 'special offer' permanently above them – not as part of the ad, but as part of the website design.

Take this example, from the Ryanair website, in which the 'special offer' is an ad from the NHS promoting an online advice service to help people give up smoking. Are they making this service even more free than before, perhaps?

How Damart got its customers overheated

DESPITE ITS CURLERS and slippers image, thermal underwear company Damart got into hot water with a mailshot sent to customers in 2005. The envelope showed it was from the 'Finance Director', said 'FINAL REMINDER' and 'ATTENTION concerning your customer file: SETTLEMENT OF OUTSTANDING ITEMS'.

Inside, the official-looking letter from the finance director had a box headlined 'ACCOUNT SETTLEMENT', gave the customer's details and the date of their first purchase from Damart.

The letter read:

Having studied your account file, and unless our letters have crossed in the post it seems that you still have available to you a number of offers that you have not yet taken up. Alison Dale has asked me to inform of you this without delay because they are still available, but only for a few more days ... Because you are such a good customer, and because you haven't taken up all the offers available to you during the season, we have extended the deadline by another 14 days ... I look forward to hearing from you very soon so that I can give the necessary instructions to my Financial department. We need to update your file quickly and to do this we need to know what you want us to do.

Making a marketing shot look like an unpaid bill drew instant complaints, particularly as many of Damart's customers are elderly. The ASA pointed out that 'recipients were likely to infer that it was a final reminder for an unpaid bill.'

Damart acknowledged that they might have misjudged the mailing, and apologised by letter and phone to all those customers who had complained.

as low as

We see low prices screaming out of stationery catalogues, accompanied by the obligatory words 'as low as'. The price shown isn't the price you pay if you only want one, though: it indicates the lowest unit price if you buy the maximum bulk quantity. The price shown is a come-on, designed to make you think a product costs less than it really does. Only if you buy far more than you need of any one item will you obtain it at this bargain rate.

E&OE

It used to be that if you saw a product advertised then the price shown was the price at which you could buy it. If a typing error meant that a video recorder was advertised at £1.99 rather than £199, then you were within your rights to claim the article for the price advertised.

This wasn't a device for purchasers to rip off retailers: rather the opposite. The law was designed to prevent shopkeepers from luring customers in with the promise of prices they then deliberately failed to fulfil.

A tricksy piece of legal chicanery, the acronym 'E&OE' closes the loophole. It stands for 'Errors and Omissions Excepted', which means that if the advertiser makes a mistake – tough luck. The typing-error bargain era is over.

The 'commission free' money that isn't

NOBODY WANTS THEIR HOLIDAY spoilt by discovering that they've been ripped off buying their foreign currency. That's why so many people are attracted by bureaux de change that offer 'zero commission', not realising that some of these places ought to have a flashing neon sign outside saying '*Suckers, this way!*'

Just because a service is offered as 'commission free' it does not mean that you're necessarily getting a good deal. On the contrary, all that's happening is that the true costs are being hidden from you. Even such companies as Thomson travel agents and the Post Office are guilty of giving poor rates. Specialist foreign exchange provider Currencies Direct conducted a survey in August 2009 and found a massive variation between the best and worst rates on offer.

At a time when Currencies Direct was itself offering to give £1,000 for €1,158, the Post Office, which offers '0% commission, competitive rates on over 70 foreign currencies', and has a respectable online exchange rate, would give just €1,094 in one of its branches, while Thomson was even worse at €1,070.

Worst culprits of all, though, were the bureaux in airports and stations. ICE at St Pancras, for instance, gave out just €1,040 for each £1,000.

It appears that the best rates come from either using specialist foreign exchange providers or buying prepaid foreign currency cards, which are like a plastic, more convenient version of travellers' cheques. The survey found one giving €1,152, meaning that somebody buying their Euros on one would be almost €50 better off for each £500 than the luckless traveller changing money at the last moment at St Pancras.

It pays to shop around and to compare online prices, using an internet service such as the Travel Money Maximiser at *www.moneysavingexpert.com*.

The camera lies: a change of view

WE DON'T ALWAYS NEED to resort to studio or digital trickery in order to make photographs tell a different story: moving the position of the camera is a simple way to change the emphasis of a scene. The Italian dictator Benito Mussolini, a notoriously short man, knew the value of low camera angles, which made him look like a taller and more imposing statesman: we look up to those who are taller than us, both figuratively and literally.

● *Making short men seem taller: Mussolini and Hitler photographed from a low angle.*

Sometimes public figures want to appear smaller than they really are. Princess Diana was a classic example: she would frequently be filmed giving interviews with her head tilted down, looking up at those to whom she was speaking. The effect was to make her appear shorter, which increased the feeling of protectiveness, particularly in male viewers.

Diana had other issues with her height, as well. The main issue was that, at 5 feet 10 inches, she was the same height as her husband, Prince Charles; and when she wore high heels she appeared taller than him. But convention dictates that the husband must be taller than his wife.

So, in portraits of the couple together, Diana was often posed lower down in the image. The official photo of Charles and Diana that accompanied their engagement announcement was taken on the steps in front of the classical façade of Highgrove, Diana carefully positioned a step or two below Charles so that he appeared to tower above her.

● *Charles towers over Diana – on the steps of Highgrove, and in the studio.*

Sometimes this technique was taken to ridiculous extremes, so Charles was made to appear a colossus beside his diminutive wife – clearly outlining who wore the trousers in the relationship.

Charles' second wife, Camilla, is only an appropriate five feet eight inches in height, so he can appear to be the boss even when she wears high heels.

We have become so inured to the tricks of photomontage

that we assume that unedited, unmanipulated photographs somehow tell the real truth: after all, this was the real scene as the photographer captured it.

But the choice of where to point the camera, where to stand, and how to arrange the subjects is as artificial as anything that could be achieved in Photoshop. Cameras never tell the whole truth: they only show what the photographer wants us to see.

ninety-nine pee

A supermarket toy costs 99p. A radio costs £9.99. A SatNav costs £99.99. Do they really think we're fooled into thinking things are cheaper than they are? Are we truly expected to fall for the 'under a pound', 'under a tenner', 'under a hundred quid' line?

Well, yes we are. We're complicit in allowing ourselves to be conned into imagining that an item costs less than it truly does, even though we know we're fooling ourselves.

But that's not how the whole thing started. Initially, the scheme was introduced in large stores to prevent cashier fraud: by forcing them to open the till to give change, the stores were preventing the cashiers from pocketing the notes.

A survey by Virgin Money reckoned that £11 million a month is wasted in customers not taking, or losing, those odd pennies. A third of those polled demanded the introduction of a 99p coin for use in such occasions.

There have been many calls for these miserable runts of coins to be consigned to history. But, as a lab technician in *The Simpsons* put it: 'If you've ever handled a penny, the government has your DNA on file. Why do you think they keep them in circulation?'

I wish I hadn't said that

'I will have failed in this if in five years there are not many more people using public transport and far fewer journeys by car. It is a tall order but I want you to hold me to it.'

John Prescott, 6 June 1997. Car traffic increased from 365.8bn vehicle kilometres in 1997 to 392.9bn in 2002. The cost of travel by public transport rose considerably.

What goes into a cheap pizza?

PIZZA EATERS THROUGHOUT the UK have been rejoicing over the low price of San Marco brand pizza, which throughout 2009 sold for as little as £1 in supermarkets such as Sainsbury, Tesco and Kwik Save.

It's certainly a bargain price for a full-size pizza, especially for their Pizza Napoli, which is helpfully described on the box as 'Deep pan pizza topped with analogue cheese, reformed ham, mushrooms and mozzarella cheese.'

'Reformed ham' is made from emulsified or chopped 'meat'. By 'meat' we don't mean *meat*, of course, but the scraps left over after all the good stuff has been packaged and sold. This may contain muscle, but is more likely to consist of 'connective tissue'. It's pumped full of water and sodium polyphosphates, which hold the water in place.

But what are we to make of 'analogue cheese'? It turns out it's a cheese substitute generally manufactured from soy or rice (the manufacturing process varies between suppliers). Originally

created for vegans who wanted to be sure their 'cheese' had absolutely no cheese in it, analogue cheese is being bought in bulk by pizza makers more interested in price than ethics.

The trouble with analogue cheese, as users point out, is that while they can make it look and smell more or less like cheese, it doesn't taste like cheese. But hey, what can you expect for a quid?

passive voice

The 'passive voice' is the grammatical construction used by someone who wishes to wriggle out of accepting responsibility for an action.

When Richard Nixon finally uttered the closest he came to an apology for the Watergate scandal, he did so with the words 'Mistakes were made'. What he didn't add was 'by me,' of course: he'd already implicitly passed the burden of blame onto someone else.

bee line

'Making a bee line' means going in a straight line towards your target. But have you ever *seen* a bee fly?

— I wish I hadn't said that —

'I meant no insult to the people of Papua New Guinea, who I'm sure lead lives of blameless bourgeois domesticity ... My remarks were inspired by a Time Life book I have which does indeed show relatively recent photos of Papua New Guinean tribes engaged in warfare, and I'm fairly certain that cannibalism was involved.'

Boris Johnson in 2006, apologising after his *Daily Telegraph* column referred to 'Papua New Guinea-style orgies of cannibalism and chief-killing'.

Creative childcare

IN 2007, TV NANNY Claire Verity was hauled in by Channel 4, for whom she'd made the series *Bringing Up Baby*, after *The Times* queried her childcare qualifications. According to her agents, 'Claire is highly qualified with a Diploma in Pre School Practice, awards in OCN Maternity Practice and Post Natal Depression, a MNT in Care of Multiple babies, a MNT in Sleep Training, a MNT in Emergency Paediatric First Aid and a MNT in Breast Feeding.'

However, Maternity Nurse Training said: 'This person never enrolled on any of our courses and as such has never been trained by us. We would like to make it quite clear that we do not in any way endorse the methods employed by Miss Verity in her work.' Verity had also claimed a Business Studies degree from York University. York does not offer a business studies degree. After an investigation, Channel 4 said that no documentary evidence of her qualifications had been produced and they would not be working with her again.

Verity's controversial approach to childcare – which included the recommendation that babies be left alone to scream, leaving them in their own room from birth, and feeding every four hours – had already caused outrage from some childcare groups.

● *Bringing up baby, but without Claire – only her hand remains*

Channel 4 still promotes the series on its website, using the same photograph it has always used. Except that now, Claire Verity (standing at the back) has been chopped out of the frame.

Cooking the records: the chef with the castle

EX-ROYAL NAVY CHEF Robert Irvine was named one of the '25 fittest guys in America'. He hosted the popular Food Network series 'Dinner: Impossible' in 2007, the station calling him 'a culinary James Bond'. But an article in Florida's *St Petersburg Times* in 2008 found that, as the Food Network put it, 'there were some embellishments and inaccuracies in his resume.'

It turns out that in calling his degree a 'B.S. In food and nutrition from Leeds University', the B.S. stood less for Bachelor of Science than Bull Shit. 'We cannot find any connection in our records between Robert and the university,' said Sarah Spiller, the University's press officer.

In his biog and his cookbook and autobiography *Mission: Cook!*, Irvine claimed to have worked on the wedding cake for Prince Charles and Princess Diana's wedding. At the Royal School of Cookery, he was assigned to 'painstakingly inspecting, culling and cleaning billions of individual bits of dried fruit . . . This was "KP" of the highest order for Queen and country.'

However Dave Avery, the chef who supervised the cake said, 'Robert Irvine may have been a trainee student at the Royal Naval Cookery School whilst I was making the royal wedding cake. He most certainly was not involved with me in making or baking the cake.'

Irvine moved to St Petersburg, Florida, in 2006 to open a couple of restaurants, saying he wanted to turn the city into 'the next Monaco'. He called himself 'Sir Robert Irvine, Knight Commander of the Royal Victorian Order,' telling people there were 'five levels of knights, and KCVO is the highest level of knight you could be. The queen handpicks you.' Unfortunately for Irvine, Buckingham palace press officer Jenn Stebbing told the *St Petersburg Times*, 'He is not a KCVO Knight Commander of the Royal Victorian Order and he wasn't given a castle by the

● *Irvine takes the biscuit.*

queen of England.' A castle? Yup. Irvine also claimed that she had given him one in Scotland.

His claims to have been a White House chef and to have cooked for Presidents Reagan, Clinton, George and G. W. Bush didn't hold up either. He did work in the Navy Mess in the West Wing, but former White House executive chef Walter Scheib said that, 'Never in the period from 1994 until 2005 did he have anything to do with the preparation, planning, or service of any State Dinner or any other White House Executive Residence food function, private or public.' Quizzed about that, Irvine said: 'I can't talk about it because it's the White House.'

St Petersburg didn't become the 'new Monaco'. Irvine's restaurants there haven't opened. However, the Food Network are clearly forgiving people. They gave him another six-part series in 2009.

full confidence

If you're a minister, hearing that the Prime Minister has 'full confidence' in you is a sure sign that the executioner is sharpening his knife and that your head is about to go onto the block. It's the same for public servants in whom ministers express 'full confidence'. You just know that you might as well clear out your desk before your pass won't let you into the building and your car parking place has somebody else's name on it.

On 28 November 2004, Tony Blair announced that he had 'full confidence' in Home Secretary David Blunkett, following revelations of his affair with a married woman. Less than three weeks later, Blunkett was out of a job.

—— I wish I hadn't said that ——

'I can't stand politicians who wear God on their sleeves.'

Tony Blair, *Sunday Telegraph,* 7 April 1996.
Blair converted to Catholicism in 2007 and set up the
Tony Blair Faith Foundation in May 2008. He told an
Italian religious conference, August 2009: 'Ever since
I began preparations to become a Catholic I felt I was
coming home and this is now where my heart is, where
I know I belong.'

The columnist who was sold a pup

RICHARD LITTLEJOHN, the *Daily Mail*'s star columnist, got his knickers in a twist about a mother in Shropshire who had given her newly-born quintuplets unusual names.

Births

PONG On 27th August 2009 to Kate Pong, Newport, Shropshire, beautiful quintuplets, Beyoncé, Tyra, Bobbi, Barack and Earl.

Littlejohn took a few paragraphs at the end of a bizarre rant about John Prescott to lay into Kate Pong, who had named her offspring Beyoncé, Tyra, Bobbi, Barack and Earl. 'My first reaction was that this must be a wind-up', he exclaimed, before asserting that 'we rang *The Times* advertising department and they assured us it was genuine.' He goes on to fume: 'There's no mention of a Mr Pong, or any father's name for that matter.'

But Littlejohn need have little cause for concern. Kate Pong, it turns out, is a chocolate labrador who gave birth to pups a couple of weeks earlier. One of her owners' friends had inserted the announcement in *The Times*.

This is just one example of how journalists frequently fail to let common sense get in the way of a good story. In the same week, the *Daily Manabzamin* – a leading Bangladeshi newspaper – reported that a conspiracy theorist had convinced Neil Armstrong, the first man to set foot on the moon, that the moon landing had in fact been a complete fake.

The story was taken up by the *New Nation* and several other newspapers, all keen to spread the word. Their source? That most reliable news agency, The Onion. No-one at the *Daily Manabzamin*, it seems, realized that The Onion was the internet's best known spoof news site. 'We thought it was true so we printed it without checking,' admitted associate editor Hasanuzzuman Khan.

Neanderthal

The word 'Neanderthal' is often used to mean uncultured and unsophisticated. But recent studies have found that the real Neanderthals, who died out around 28,000 years ago, were actually pretty bright for the time and, according to Dr Terry Hopkinson of Leicester University, were adept at innovation and using tools to work stone. They even conjured up an early form of superglue to fasten a flint blade to a wooden shaft, using pitch which had to be heated to over 300°C.

Not quite so stupid after all, then.

mammoth

The word 'mammoth' is widely used to mean something immense. After all, mammoths were enormous, weren't they, even bigger than modern elephants?

In fact, they weren't as big as people imagine. Although a few examples of really big mammoths have been found, the average one was about the same size as a modern Asian or Indian elephant and they aren't as big as African elephants. So that mammoth task you were dreading probably isn't quite as monumental as you thought.

'For the past 20 years, I've been polishing my CV'

EVERYBODY THINKS they could write a novel, if only they had the time. But according to employers, many CVs already qualify as works of fiction. A study by CareerBuilder.com found that while just 5% of people looking for work admitted to lying on their resumés, managers responsible for hiring put the figure at 57%. Someone might exaggerate their experience, education or qualifications, say they were in a position longer than they really were or not mention that they were sacked from a job.

Many firms will withdraw job offers if they discover fibs that are too outrageous, or even sack people once they are employed. One of the spectacular CV fibbers was Neil Taylor, the £115,000 per annum head of the Shrewsbury and Telford Hospitals NHS Trust. He found himself in court in 2003 after it was discovered that he wasn't in fact a graduate, as he had claimed to be.

Judge Onions went on to tell him, 'It seems to me that people who lie about qualifications undermine the effort of everybody who goes through a course and obtains a proper qualification . . . what's the point of me studing law for three years if I can just invent the degree?'

For Alison Ryan, becoming Director of Communications at Manchester United in 1999 on a salary of £125,000 p.a. was a 'dream come true'. She never got as far as her new office. Before her first day, the truth came out that she didn't have a first in history from Cambridge, had faked her references, hadn't achieved a distinction in her law exam, and had even been debarred by the Bar Council.

In 2006 David Edmondson, Chief Executive of Radio Shack, resigned after a paper revealed that he had fibbed about getting degrees in theology and psychology. Clearly he wasn't that bright, as the Pacific Coast Baptist College never offered psychology as a subject. Commenting on the story, business ethics professor

Ronald Simms said that this sort of lie snowballs over time as the person has to lie to cover the original fabrication. 'I've seen people who forgot what they put on their resumés. Some people actually convince themselves that they earned degrees they lied about before.'

Research by the Risk Advisory Group found 65% of CVs with false information. The worst culprits were women in their early 30s, 77% of whom told whoppers of some sort. But even half of the men in their early 20s, the most honest group, embellished the truth. The company is a new breed of firm, common in America, which check the CVs of potential employees – sort of CV detectives.

However, for every employer who says it doesn't pay to lie on your CV, there's somebody in a job who knows that if they hadn't shaved a few years off their age, or failed to mention their bouts of depression or that they were trying for a baby, they wouldn't have been told 'you're hired'.

Pterodactlyls *can* fly

Lee McQueen, the pterodactyl-impersonating 'Apprentice' winner in 2009, was discovered to have fibbed on his CV. Instead of spending two years at Thames Valley University, he had left after just four months. There was much sanctimonious tutting that Sir Alan Sugar decided to employ McQueen anyway.

Sugar reckoned: 'Every single person out there has lied on their CV. This whole thing has been blown out of all proportion.' He confessed to a reporter there was a game he liked to play with himself, 'When some of the so-called high-flying executives who work for me leave because they decide that the grass is greener somewhere else, I like to have some fun by getting their CVs sent back to me, just so that I see what they've said – "located a factory myself" or "designed a new range of computers". A pack of lies. It's what people do.'

So noisy was the row that even the Prime Minister waded in. Gordon Brown said that, while he did not agree with lying, 'we should support [him] in his decision'.

Unlike Sir Alan Sugar, however, 93% of employers are said not to hire people they later discover to have lied on their CV. Presumably they've all forgotten how they got their job in the first place.

So who's doing the faking?

The employee screening company Powerchex conducted a survey of nearly 4,000 job applications submitted to financial institutions, and found that students from some backgrounds and disciplines were more likely to embellish their CVs than others. Among the findings were:

- 43% of students from former polytechnics fib on their applications, compared with 14% from leading universities.

- 22% of arts and humanities students fake their CVs, compared with 6% of students who took mathematics degrees.

- Job applicants from the UK were more likely to falsify their CVs than those from any other country.

Sorry really is
the hardest word

IN JAPAN, if an official or businessman made a grievous mistake, the traditional way of apologising was to commit hara kiri. Here, in the past, falling on one's sword was rather less deadly: the honourable thing to do was to apologise and resign. Disgraced minister John Profumo, for instance, admitted to committing what was then the most heinous of crimes – lying to the House of Commons. He retired from public life and dedicated his remaining years to charitable causes.

How times have changed. Now those in authority are so contemptuous of the public that not only won't they resign without being pushed, but they won't even apologise. Take Des Browne, Defence Secretary in 2007 when Royal Navy sailors were not only captured by Iran but then allowed to sell their stories to the newspapers. With the House baying for an apology, Browne would only say, 'I have expressed a degree of regret which I think can be equated with an apology.' When that still wasn't enough, he grudgingly went on, 'If you want me to say "sorry", then I am happy to say "sorry".' But he didn't.

Although Tony Blair apologised for the Irish potato famine and the slave trade (see page 218), he wouldn't do so over Iraq: 'I have searched my conscience, not in a spirit of obstinacy, but in genuine reconsideration . . . for any mistakes [made] in good faith I of course take full responsibility.'

So rare is it for a politician to apologise these days that, when it does happen, it is news. After President-elect Obama's nominee for Health and Human Services Secretary, Tom Daschle, was found not to have paid all his back taxes, Obama astonished everyone by saying, 'It is a mess and it's my responsibility . . . I've screwed up and I want to tell the people of this country that I'm sorry.' The plaudits he received for taking the blame made no difference to our own politicians, presumably afraid that saying 'sorry' was seen as a sign of weakness. As the MPs' expenses scandal continued through the spring and summer of 2009, very few apologies seemed in the least bit heartfelt. Rather, MPs seemed aggrieved that the gravy train had been derailed:

- 'I bitterly regret the system' and 'I am sorry we have all become embroiled in this expenses row, particularly as I was following advice.' Husband and wife MPs Andrew MacKay and Julie Kirkbride, who nominated two properties as 'second homes' so they could claim for both.

- 'I have acted in complete good faith and within the rules. It is an error, which obviously I wish hadn't happened.' Jack Straw, MP for Blackburn and Justice Secretary, who claimed for a full council tax reimbursement despite getting a 50% discount.

- Andy Burnham, the culture secretary, said his claim for a £19.99 IKEA bathrobe was 'a genuine mistake', as apparently was Michael Ancram's claim of £100 for having his swimming pool repaired. Of his other claims, none 'could be considered extravagant or luxurious'.

- 'I do believe there were one or two occasions where I spent more money than I should have. People are right to be angry about the current system.' Michael Gove, who claimed a £500 hotel bill and £7,000 for furnishings.

- 'The claims were an error of judgment on my part.' James Arbuthnot, after claiming for having his swimming pool cleaned.

- Shahid Malik, the minister who had the highest expenses claim of any MP, said that his claims were 'one million per cent by the book' and that he did not get a 'good service' from the Commons Fees Office because they didn't advise him there was an upper limit imposed on individual claims.

- 'The fact is that these allowances would not have been paid if they weren't within the rules.' Lord Mandelson, who claimed for work on a property he did up after announcing that he was standing down from Parliament.

- 'The claims were made within House of Commons rules which were designed to reflect the fact that MPs have to meet the cost of living in two places.' Chancellor Alistair Darling, who 'flipped' his second home designation four times to boost the amounts he could claim on each.

- 'That was a mistake. It should not have been made.' Former minister Margaret Beckett explaining on 'Question Time', amid booing, why she'd claimed £600 for plants and hanging baskets, though omitting to mention there had been three near-identical claims in the past.

- When Sir Menzies Campbell apologised on the same 'Question Time', he said that claiming for his interior designer was obviously wrong. Asked why he hadn't known it was wrong at the time he said, 'The public perceptions at the time were quite different.'

'In good faith', 'genuine mistake', 'one million per cent by the book', 'the system', 'error of judgment', 'within the rules', 'following advice.' And they wonder why the public are so angry with them. If saying 'sorry' were all that were required, our prisons would be empty.

As Professor John Haldane of St Andrews University pointed out, 'People are often willing to say things that meet the demands of having to issue an apology . . . which means they are not fully 'fessing up to the whole thing. That's partly because they know it will cost them if they do.'

It isn't only politicians, of course. When Russell Brand and Jonathan Ross left explicit messages on Andrew Sachs's answerphone in late 2008 about Brand having had sex with his granddaughter, Brand 'apologised' on air, after his own fashion. 'I'd like to take this opportunity to issue a personal Russell Brand apology to Andrew Sachs, the great comic actor who played Manuel, for a message that Jonathan and I left on his answerphone, but it was quite funny. But, sometimes you mustn't swear on someone's answerphone and that's why I'd like to apologise personally.'

Of course, insincere apologies are nothing new. The 18th-century playwright Richard Sheridan, for instance, once had to apologise in the House of Commons for calling a fellow MP a liar: 'Mr Speaker, I said the Honourable member was a liar it is true and I am sorry for it. The Honourable member may place the punctuation where he pleases.'

● *Sheridan: a skilled apologiser*

Come friendly immigrants and drop on Slough

MANY OF US ARE SCEPTICAL at the flow of statistics that supposedly prove that life is getting better in every way. But most of us have no way of challenging official numbers, however bizarre they may appear.

In 2007, Slough Council reckoned that faulty statistics would see them being underfunded by £15m, for they showed that the Berkshire town's population was declining rapidly.

This made no sense at all to the council. The death rate was going down and the birth rate was going up, as were the number of people paying council tax and applying for National Insurance numbers. In just 18 months, the Council had to find places for 900 children of migrants arriving in the town. Council leader Richard Stokes said that Government figures on migration were 'not fit for purpose'.

Slough and three other councils complained to the Treasury, saying that a new method of calculating immigration figures, the so-called 'Improved Methods for Population Statistics Revisions' was giving 'perverse results'. They showed, for instance, that London's migrant population was 60,000 less than the previous estimate, even though, according to Simon Milton, leader of Westminster City Council, 2,000 migrants arrive at Victoria Coach Station each week. The councils said the figures didn't 'remotely' chime with their experience.

Stephen Greenhalgh, leader of Hammersmith and Fulham Council, said: 'I didn't think it was possible but this new method for counting migration is actually worse than the old one – which was also a disaster. In 2004, Britain was one of only three countries giving full work rights to citizens of the new Eastern European EU countries. The Home Office forecast a maximum of 13,000 migrants a year. By 2007, one million had arrived. In 2009, figures from the Office for National Statistics showed

that 6.5 million people living in Britain in 2007 had been born abroad, a rise of 21 per cent in just three years. Phil Woolas, the Immigration Minister, accused the ONS of 'sinister' motives for releasing the data, dismissing their projections of a UK of 70 million by 2031.

Government fiddling of migration figures is a major headache for councils as they receive £600 for each 'official' inhabitant, but have to provide education and health facilities for everyone living there.

Merrick Cockell, the head of Kensington and Chelsea Council, said, 'This loss of funding will put a considerable strain on our ability to provide the excellent services we pride ourselves on.'

As for Slough, just to prove how wrong the Government figures were, they measured the town's flow of sewage and found that it had increased by over 10% in just one year.

You can't argue with shit.

Sat navs ate my hamster, and other nonsense

ANYONE WHO HAS USED a satellite navigation system in their car will know that, occasionally, the maps can be out of date. But they're likely to be far more current than old-fashioned paper maps, and at least they can be updated over the internet.

Occasionally, sat navs will make mistakes in guidance. When a sat nav suggests a route that leads down a road that's clearly far too narrow, rather than using their common sense, drivers are all too willing to follow the spoken directions – despite the fact that the route is clearly unsuitable.

Among the more ludicrous stories reported in the press are:

- The 10-year-old girl who was left bleeding and vomiting in the street after being hit by a car, having to wait 32 minutes for an ambulance to arrive. On the way to the hospital the girl's mother told the driver of a better route, who insisted they had to follow the sat nav. The journey took 40 minutes, compared with the 22 minutes a more direct route would have taken.

- A party of pensioners going for a pub lunch in the Forest of Dean were left stranded for four hours when their coach tried to follow a route down a country lane that was clearly impassable for such a large vehicle.

- A group of school children going to Hampton Court Palace found themselves in Hampton Court, Islington, after the coach driver blindly followed directions to a location 17 miles from Henry VIII's palace. 'You would have thought one would have checked on a map before they left,' said a disgruntled parent.

- The Christmas outing for Cheltenham and Gloucester workers, which was supposed to take place in Lille, France – but the driver drove to a town of the same name in Belgium

- A 47-year-old driver who had to spend the night in the cab of his 17.5 tonne truck rather than attend his son's 18th birthday party, because his sat nav had got him stuck in a muddy country lane.

- The Belgian truck driver who caused £20,000 worth of damage driving over a car and wrecking five others, after he got trapped in a cul-de-sac.

- The motorist Satlegh Mohammadi, who drove his Ford Fiesta for 20 feet along a railway line.

- The taxi driver who took Earl Spencer's daughter, Katya, to a football match at Stamford Bridge – but chose the Stamford Bridge in North Yorkshire, rather than the Chelsea ground.

- The taxi driver in Swaffham, Norfolk, who got stuck after driving 200 yards up a river bed.

- Paula Ceely of Worcester, who was given a route that involved her opening a large metal gate across the road. 'The sat nav insisted it was the correct way so I opened it and drove through,' she told the *Daily Telegraph*. Only the sound of a train horn alerted her to the fact that she was standing on a railway line. 'I'll never use a sat nav again,' she avowed.

A British Transport Police spokesman, commenting on the Paula Ceely incident, said: 'We would advise people to use sat navs with due caution.' In other words, don't be so idiotic and use a bit of common sense.

Once in a while, stupidity with sat nav use can be in the public good. Such was the case with the gang of armed robbers in Hampshire, who were arrested after a series of bank raids, and convicted largely on the evidence of the driver's sat nav: he'd entered a dozen banks into the device as 'places of interest'.

pre-enjoyed

It used to be that we talked about 'second hand' or 'used' cars. Then someone figured out that 'used' made it sound like it was all used up, and 'second hand' sounded like the previous owner didn't want it any more (which they didn't).

So we got 'pre-owned' cars instead, which just sounds as if someone happened to own the car temporarily before you did, but it's still your new car. That was all very well, until 'pre-enjoyed' came along. Now, the implication is that someone else has spent their ownership doing nothing other than preparing the car for your future enjoyment, breaking it in, as it were, teasing it to the very peak of enjoyability for your ultimate delectation.

The phrase has so far been largely confined to the United States, but there it's gained so much currency that people just accept it without a second thought: take this entry on the networking site Spoke.com from Bruce Mcdonald of Strongs Marine, who describes himself as a 'Pre-Enjoyed Sales Manager'. Crumbs!

I wish I hadn't said that

'My comments do not accurately reflect my views.'

Licensing Minister Gerry Sutcliffe, after a ticking-off for stating that 'we, and I speak as a champion of the pub trade, want the Chancellor to change his mind' on an increase in the duty on beer and wine.

And now a question from the audience…

WHEN JOHN PHILBIN, head of PR for the Federal Emergency Management Agency, held a televised news briefing following the California wildfires in 2007, it was to be one of his last engagements before taking over as media chief for the US director of national intelligence.

But Philbin had screwed up the process of inviting reporters to the Fema press conference, with the result that while the TV crews had turned up, journalists could only access the meeting by phone, in listen-in mode and with no opportunity for them to ask questions.

With no reporters present, but a barrage of TV cameras, Philbin had arranged for Fema staff to ask the questions instead. Tricky, penetrating questions, such as, 'Are you happy with Fema's response so far?'

'My mistake,' admitted Philbin.

Mike McConnell, the US director of national intelligence, was not amused: Philbin lost the job before he'd even started. 'We can confirm that Mr Philbin is not, nor is he scheduled to be, the director of public affairs,' said his office.

It's not the first time questions have been planted in the audience. While battling Barack Obama for the Democratic presidential nomination at a meeting before the important Iowa caucus, Hillary Clinton called on a student in the audience for a question. Muriel Gallo-Chasanoff duly asked how the senator intended to fight climate change.

'You know,' Senator Clinton glowingly replied, 'I find as I travel around Iowa that it's usually young people that ask me about global warming.'

The student later admitted that she'd been fed the question in advance by a member of Clinton's staff, who then pointed her out to the candidate.

Sleazy come, sleazy go

BELIEVE IT OR NOT, there is actually a code of conduct for MPs. The latest version, dated June 2009, says that:

> *In carrying out their parliamentary and public duties, Members will be expected to observe the following general principles of conduct.*

These are grouped into the categories of Selflessness, Integrity, Objectivity, Accountability, Openness, Honesty and Leadership.

Although it may bring forth hollow laughter after the MPs' expenses scandal, MPs swear to:

- 'take decisions solely in terms of the public interest. They should not do so in order to gain financial or other material benefits for themselves, their family, or their friends.'

- be 'accountable for their decisions and actions to the public and must submit themselves to whatever scrutiny is appropriate to their office.'

- 'be as open as possible about all the decisions and actions that they take'.

- 'give reasons for their decisions and restrict information only when the wider public interest clearly demands.'

In 1999, Elizabeth Filkin was appointed Parliamentary Commissioner for Standards, her job being to ensure that MPs followed the rules and to root out any wrongdoing among our Parliamentarians. According to Peter Oborne in his book *The Triumph of the Political Class*, she exposed a 'shocking pattern of arrogance, corruption, greed, bullying and deception among ministers, ordinary MPs and leading figures from the Conservative opposition.'

She upset MPs with what they saw as overzealousness, ruling for instance that Cabinet minister Peter Mandelson had misled his building society and Parliament by failing to declare a £373,000 loan from colleague Geoffrey Robinson and investigating the abuse of taxpayers' money by minister John Reid over the use of parliamentary researchers, one of them being his own son.

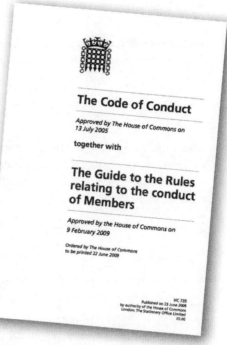

Filkin was, in effect, hounded from her job with politicians of all parties either taking part directly in the campaign against her or else colluding by saying nothing. Oborne, who has written about politics for many years, said he found it 'one of the most morally disgusting episodes I have witnessed . . . It is essentially the story of how MPs destroyed the reputation of a woman emphatically not because she had done anything wrong, but because she was too assiduous in doing her duty.'

If they had let her continue in her job of weeding out corruption and dodging dealing in Parliament, it is probable that the MPs' expenses scandal of 2009 might never have happened. It is comforting to think that some of those who sought to oust Filkin from her role as Parliamentary sleaze watchdog have now had their political careers terminated in turn.

Dishonourable members

WATCHING MPS WRIGGLE and try to justify their expense claims was one of the most entertaining sights of 2009. What should not be forgotten, however, is the way in which so many 'Honourable' Members did their utmost to ensure that the people who elected them knew as little about the expenses they had claimed as possible. The Fees Office, which governed the system, was given no power of investigation or censure by MPs and had to take expense claims on trust, a rather different way of doing things than for employees in the real world.

2005: the investigation begins

In January 2005, *Telegraph* journalist Ben Leapman used the Freedom of Information Act 2000, which had just become law – though more watered down than originally envisaged – to ask to see the Additional Costs Allowance expenses of six MPs, the ACA being the maximum annual £24,000 that MPs outside

London can claim to help run their second homes. He heard nothing for months. Then his request was rejected. He tried again. It was rejected again. So, in April, he appealed to the Information Commissioner, Richard Thomas, whose website trumpets that we all have 'the right to obtain information held by public authorities unless there are good reasons to keep it confidential.'

2007: MPs block disclosure

Nervousness among MPs led to Tory David Maclean proposing a Private Member's Bill in May 2007 to amend the FOI and exempt MPs from its regulations, ostensibly in order to cut costs and trivial queries, but in reality to stop the public learning the truth. It failed. After two whole years considering Leapman's requests, in June 2007 the Information Commissioner suggested a compromise; claims could be lumped into categories (so much on household items, so much on food, etc), but without any details or receipts because that would 'invade the privacy' of MPs.

The Commons authorities, led by leader of the house Jack Straw and the speaker Michael Martin, thought that even that was too much and appealed to the Information Tribunal. Big mistake.

2008: the scent of victory

The Information Tribunal also considered FOI requests from *The Sunday Times* and FOI campaigner Heather Brooke. They ruled in February 2008 in favour of disclosure, saying that the expenses claims of 14 MPs, including Tony Blair and Gordon Brown, should be published in full within 28 days, together with the receipts.

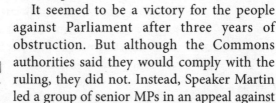

It seemed to be a victory for the people against Parliament after three years of obstruction. But although the Commons authorities said they would comply with the ruling, they did not. Instead, Speaker Martin led a group of senior MPs in an appeal against the requests to the High Court. The Speaker forbade MPs from raising the case in the House because it was *sub judice*.

All this was around the same time that it was discovered that £1.7m had been spent on Martin's official residence in just seven years, and that the Parliamentary Commissioner for Standards was investigating whether Martin himself had abused parliamentary expenses and allowances, with over £4,000 claimed in taxi trips by his wife on shopping trips and official Air Miles being used to pay for the flights of family members.

Despite Parliament incurring £150,000 in legal expenses, in May 2008 the judges sided with the tribunal: 'We are not here dealing with idle gossip, or public curiosity about what in truth are trivialities. The expenditure of public money through the payment of MPs' salaries and allowances is a matter of direct and reasonable interest to taxpayers.'

Expenses for 14 MPs covering 2001-4 were released, but all other MPs' receipts for the same period were then destroyed. These included some of Tony Blair's requested receipts, which were shredded while the request was still under consideration. This was, apparently, a 'mistake'.

The Information Tribunal and the judges agreed that MPs' addresses should be included with the information. Many MPs objected. Linking addresses to claims, of course, meant we might  discover not just the parsimious and grasping nature of so many MPs, but that many were claiming for properties they didn't live in, paying subsidied 'rent' to relatives and 'flipping' their second homes to do up one place on expenses and then flipping it back to do up the other, all paid for by the taxpayer.

As a total of one million receipts were prepared for disclosure in the summer of 2008, Tory Julian Lewis led a fight to keep MPs' addresses secret in the interests of 'security'. Parliament had no problem with that, deciding – despite the rulings of the Tribunal and the High Court – that MPs' addresses should not after all be covered by the Freedom of Information Act that *they* had only just brought into law. In November, the full publication of a million receipts covering four years was announced. And then postponed.

2009: full disclosure

In January 2009, the leader of the Commons, Harriet Harman, attempted again – and failed – to have MPs' expenses exempted from the FOI. Plaudits should be given to those MPs who opposed this, among them Kate Hoey, Jo Swinson, Peter Bottomley and Frank Field. But even with this failure, the public would not be given the full details of MPs' expenses, for they were being allowed to censor, or 'redact', the details of their million pages of expenses in advance of them being made public.

Then, on 8 May 2009, a day that felt almost as if we were reading The Washington Post on the day Woodward and Bernstein broke the Watergate scandal, the *Daily Telegraph* began publishing the full, uncensored, details of MPs expenses. Over the following days, more and more details emerged, in a mind-boggling stream of information. Many MPs were outraged. Some even demanded that the police investigate the leak. In June, a full

year after the High Court ruled that MPs should not be exempt from the FOI regulations, the redacted expenses were finally released. Comparing them to the uncensored expense claims, we were able to see that 'redacting' meant blacking out anything in the least bit incriminating or embarrassing. The fact that so much was crossed out at the request of individual MPs was far more enlightening than if the expenses had emerged unblemished.

Despite public anger, at the time of writing, many MPs are still bleating about ill-treatment. Labour MP Eric Illsley believes they should not have to submit receipts: 'This makes MPs into petty accounting clerks.' Lib Dem MP Nick Harvey defended MPs profiting from house sales where the mortgage interest had been paid by the taxpayer, saying, 'It is a victimless crime, because it does not add in any way to the taxpayers' burden.' Tory frontbencher Alan Duncan was sacked after saying that MPs were being 'forced to live on rations' and 'treated like shit'.

With delicious irony, it became clear in September 2009 why the expenses had been leaked. Many of those who were working on censoring the expenses were, in fact, active servicemen. They were moonlighting in order to pay for better equipment such as body armour and boots. Unsurprisingly, they weren't best pleased to see how MPs were featherbedding their nests while troops they had starved of proper equipment were being killed and maimed. It was, apparently, their justifiable anger that persuaded the mole to act.

The expenses themselves

In March 2009, it was revealed that MPs' expenses for the previous year – all tax free – totalled £93m, an average of £144,000 each on top of their salaries of £64,766 and upwards. Half of them claimed within 10% of the maximum second homes allowance – homes on which we, the public, were paying the Council tax. Bear in mind that only 'essential' items could legally be claimed for. Claims included:

- £1,645 for a duck house (Sir Peter Viggers)
- £7.99 for a book called *Reasons to be Cheerful* and £300 for 500 posters of himself (Ed Balls)
- £10 for the porn films watched by the husband of the Home Secretary (Jacqui Smith)
- £22,500 for treating her boyfriend's dry rot, 100 miles from her constituency (Margaret Moran)
- 39p for a single paper clip (Bob Blizzard)
- £25,000 for private security patrols (multi-millionaire tourism minister Barbara Follett)
- £47 for two copies of a DVD of his own speech on 'Value for Taxpayers' Money' (George Osborne)
- 38p for a Muller Crunch Corner yoghurt and £1.06 for an Asda Pizza for his assistant (Shaun Woodward, the wealthiest member of the Labour cabinet)
- £500,000 expenses to Sinn Fein MPs who have never taken their seats
- 77p for a light bulb and £1.65 for shampoo (Adrian Bailey).

There were expenses for swimming pools, cleaning moats, tennis courts, nannies, light bulbs, TV licences, a 26p wooden spoon, a Kit-kat, a 5p plastic bag, tampons, a jar of Branston pickle, pork pies, jellied eels, horse manure, silk cushions, fancy dress wigs, £1,600 for window cleaning, iPods, a trouser press, a bath plug, washing machines, £16.50 for a Royal British Legion wreath, a flatscreen TV, hedge trimming, the refitting of a toilet seat (John Prescott, twice in two years), an MP's husband's life insurance, and cleaning the home of their parents. On and on the list of 'essential' items goes.

65 MPs, a tenth of the total, claimed expenses for a second home while renting out a third. Many spent the maximum £400 a month on food that is allowed without supplying receipts. Some told the Commons' authorities that one place was their second home to qualify for expenses, while telling the Inland Revenue it was the primary residence to avoid Capital Gains Tax. Many had goods for the second home, for which they were allowed expenses, delivered to their main home.

When Harry Cohen was found to have claimed a caravan as his main home, so that he could claim £300,000 'second home' expenses on a house in his constituency, he said, 'It really is part of my salary in all but name, that is what it exists for. When MPs were given this allowance they were told "Go and spend it, boys" and that is what I have done. It is my right.'

At the time, the Department for Work and Pensions was running a campaign targetting benefit fraud, which read: 'Deliberately withholding information that affects your claim is stealing ... those who steal benefits are picking the pockets of law-abiding taxpayers.' But while benefit cheats may face the full force of the law, even the most egregious MPs have been given no more than smacks on their naughty wrists and allowed to retire with staggeringly generous pensions.

£112.52

Hoof hearted

'**AS THEY COME TO THE TURN**, it's Far Kinnel by a neck, followed by Noble Ox, Betty Swallocks, Wear the Fox Hat and, bringing up the rear, Drew Peacock.'

Alas, it's rare for racing commentators be forced to get their mouths around such verbal plums. It may be the Sport of Kings but horse owners are constantly trying to deceive the censors of the sport and slip in naughty names for their runners. The names of the 15,000 thoroughbred horses registered in Britain each year have been carefully vetted for centuries by the Jockey Club, and more recently by Weatherbys.

Weatherbys shed light on some of the suggested racehorse names that don't make it. They know instantly to check anything containing Ophelia or Norfolk (Norfolk and Chance would stand no chance at all) and Welsh-looking names such as Llamedos or Llareggub are almost certainly trying it on. Among those they rejected were Beau Lux Blair, Wear the Fox Hat, Far Kinnel, Noble Ox, Drew Peacock and Betty Swallocks.

As trainer John Best's stables are in Hucking, many of his horses sound rude, like Hucking Hero and Hucking Heist. A horse called Selosra ran a few races, though presumably not backwards, while, in the same vein, there was a gelding Aussie horse called Stun On. In Australia in 2008, a horse achieved notoriety after just one race. Aydee Fic, as Racing Information Services Australia soon found out, is rather a rude phrase in Arabic. The horse's name had to be changed after it won its debut race at Toowoomba.

France, too, has to be careful. In 2003, the Prix des Favourites, run at Longchamp, saw 12 horses pass the finishing post. The ninth was called Big Tits. Trainer Elie Lellouche said they were trying to come up with names at a family lunch and his son jokingly suggested Gros Nichons. 'That wouldn't have got past France Galop so we decided on the English equivalent.' *The Sun* delighted in reporting that, thanks to a reciprocal arrangement, if Big Tits wanted to run in Britain, the authorities would have to allow it. Sadly, the horse appears to have spent its life in France.

Among horses that *have* run here, and in other counties, are the gelding (obviously) Noble Locks, Roger the Butler, Shiitake, Titsan, My Aunt Fanny and Katchit. Amazingly, famous trainer Julie Cecil had a horse spooneristically named Mary Hinge which won five races, picking up over £25,000 in prize money.

We were sceptical, but all can be checked in an online thoroughbred database that gives you their lineage. Noble Locks, which ran in the USA, for instance, was born in 1998 out of Night Shift and Imperial Graf. And while the UK authorities may have been wise to it, the Americans permitted a 2006 filly to be named Wear the Fox Hat.

The delightfully-named Hoof Hearted runs today in South Africa, with earlier horses by the same name in France in the 90s, and in America in the 80s. There's actually footage from a 1989 American horse race on YouTube with the commentator getting terribly excited as

Hoof Hearted heads for the post, a clip which ends with him yelling: 'Hoof Hearted in the winner's circle'.

Who indeed?

probably

In 1974 the advertising agency Saatchi & Saatchi came up with the line 'Carlsberg. Probably the best beer in the world.' Like many Saatchi catchphrases, it was a work of genius: while the bald statement 'the best beer in the world' would lay Carlsberg open to all sorts of counter claims and possible advertising standards infringements, the qualifier 'probably' gave them the perfect get-out clause.

As anyone who has tasted Carlsberg will know, of course, the claim isn't true. Probably.

allegedly

A word popularised by the satirical news quiz *Have I Got News for You*, and the show's equivalent of Carlsberg's 'probably'. Apparently, though, this is no defence against libel, and may even make matters worse as it implies that you doubt the truth of the statement you've just uttered.

Allegedly.

I wish I hadn't said that

'I think I have behaved impeccably. I have done nothing criminal. And you know what it's about? Jealousy. I have got a very, very large house . . . What right does the public have to interfere in my private life? None.'

Anthony Steen MP, after it was revealed that the interfering public had paid over £87,000 for on the upkeep of his constituency mansion, which he had designated a second home. Claims included charges for rabbit fencing, tree surgery and woodland consultants.

Free and fair

POLITICIANS OF ALL STRIPES have become ever more adept at talking without actually saying anything concrete. Sometimes, however, despite all their weasel words, they still slip up and say something that can be disproven.

In July and August 2009, British forces suffered heavy casualties taking the Babaji area in southern Afghanistan back from the Taliban, aiming to allow a possible 80,000 possible electors to cast a vote in the elections. It was a difficult operation. 10 British service personnel were killed and an estimated 150 wounded in action. There was anger in the UK when the BBC revealed that only 150 people turned up to vote even though over 4,000 votes had been counted.

Foreign Secretary David Miliband was interviewed by Ed Stourton on the 'Today Programme'. With as many casualties as legitimate votes and clear evidence of electoral fraud, Stourton wanted to know if there could ever be a credible government in Afghanistan. Miliband replied, 'We have never used the phrase "free and fair elections" because that is really not appropriate to [that] country.'

However, on 10 July 2009, Gordon Brown, the Prime Minister, said at the G8 summit in Italy: 'Our resolve to complete the work that we have started in Afghanistan is undiminished. We must help deliver a free and fair presidential election in Afghanistan.'

It's true that we could find no instance of Miliband himself using that exact phrase. In the *Financial Times* on 26 July, he wrote: 'That explains the importance of credible elections next month'; while in a speech at NATO headquarters the following day, he said, 'the elections on 20 August need to be both credible and inclusive.'

Does Miliband think that an election can be said to be 'credible' if it's neither free nor fair?

Bang to rights: is this a unfair cop?

SURELY THE POLICE should come near the top of the list of the bodies you expect to tell the truth. And yet they were caught out telling massive porkies in April 2009 after the protests against the G20 meeting in London. Leaving work, newspaper vendor Ian Tomlinson got funnelled by police into the demonstration and died. A City of London Police spokesman said that day that the police had responded to a member of the public reporting that a man 'had collapsed'. They sent medics who called for support. 'The officers took the decision to move him as during this time a number of missiles – believed to be bottles – were being thrown at them.' However, video from a passer-by showed that only one bottle had been thrown. And it missed.

The report also said: 'A post-mortem examination . . . found he died of natural causes. He suffered a sudden heart attack while on his way home from work.' The same video footage also revealed that, far from being nowhere near the police when he 'collapsed', a police officer had hit Mr Tomlinson with a baton and pushed him over for no discernible reason.

A full week later, the Independent Police Complaints Commission took over the inquiry from the very police forces whose officers were involved. Its chairman Nick Hardwick told Channel Four News that the police were hampered by not having any CCTV footage, because there were no camera in the area. Then it turned out that there were. However, it was said that Nick Hardwick hadn't apparently realised this, so believed he was speaking the truth. A second post mortem exam, carried out on behalf of the IPCC, found that Ian Tomlinson died from internal bleeding. When this book went to press, the IPCC had delivered its report, but the details were still unknown.

Sadly, this is not the only instance of the police being less than honest with the public. When in 2005 Jean Charles de Menezes

● *Ian Tomlinson, knocked to the ground by a police officer with a baton.*

was shot dead by officers in Stockwell tube station, believing him to be a suicide bomber, they claimed they shouted 'armed police' first. All the underground passengers contradicted this and the jury believed them.

In 2008, environmentalists protesting near the Kingsnorth power station in Kent argued that the 1,500-strong police operation there, which had cost £6m, was heavy-handed. The police response was to point out that 70 officers had been injured in the course of their duties. Home Office minister Vernon Coaker said in a parliamentary debate that, despite hundreds of complaints, the police had acted 'appropriately and proportionately'. The protest had clearly turned into an appalling attack on our guardians of law enforcement.

A Freedom of Information request uncovered a slightly different picture. Just 12 injuries had been reported. Only four involved another person and the protesters were not responsible for any of them. The other injuries included such life-threatening situations as 'officer succumbed to sun and heat', being 'stung on finger by possible wasp' and 'officer injured sitting in car'. The police also suffered grievously from cases of headaches, toothache, insects, diarrhoea and cut fingers, with one officer cutting his arm on a fence when climbing over it while another 'used leg to open door and next day had pain in lower back'.

The police are obliged to wear their shoulder identification numbers while on front-line work. After all, how else can they be identified if there is a subsequent inquiry. Yet, during the G20 protests, it was pointed out that some officers were concealing their collar numbers. A subsequent investigation revealed that almost half of all officers in the country surveyed did not display their identification. That included the officer who pushed Ian Tomlinson over.

Shock and Ore

The police were also guilty of appallingly misguided and blinkered behaviour during Operation Ore. Almost 4,000 British men were caught up in this investigation into child pornography which originated in America. Some no doubt deserved everything that was coming to them.

However, many were clearly victims of identity theft. All websites of the UK's police forces warn about identity theft, which the FBI calls America's 'fastest growing crime'. In the original American Operation Avalanche, 100 men were charged out of a total of 35,000 people suspected. The FBI actually thought it sensible to check whether the subscribers had used their own credit cards to join the paedophile website Landslide.

Yet in Britain, out of 7,250 suspects, 1,848 men were arrested. It appears never to have occurred to the police – or they chose to ignore the possibility – that somebody who subscribed to a website several times in one day but never actually visited it might possibly have had their identity stolen.

It made no difference if their computers showed no evidence whatsoever of child pornography or if they could prove that they had been nowhere near their computers at the time the transaction was made. It ought to be obvious that crooks skimming credit cards will know that there is little likelihood of somebody complaining to their credit card company of the police if their card has been used to subscribe to a sickening website. Not, apparently, to the police.

As far as Plod was concerned, the owners of the credit cards were the guilty ones, not the people who actually visited the website. Ross Anderson, professor of security engineering at Cambridge University, said: 'Operation Ore I think will go down as one of the worst police scandals in history . . . The police just didn't look for and didn't understand the evidence of wholesale card fraud. And as a result, hundreds of people, possibly in the low thousands of people, have been put through a terrible mill with threats of prosecution for child pornography.'

Eventually, after the protests became too vocal to ignore, they did actually check. Only then was it discovered that there were 54,348 instances of stolen credit card information in the database of the Landslide website. Even then, this information was not given to the defendants. The police tried smearing the expert computer witness they'd employed to help them, claiming that he had child pornography on the very computer he was using to assist in the case. They were later told their search was illegal.

Despite mounting evidence that the police had blundered on a massive scale, Jim Gamble, head of the Child Exploitation and Online Protection Centre, said: 'We have dealt with over 2,400 cases, over 90% of the individuals involved pleaded guilty – that's nothing about credit card fraud.' However, many of the accused, despite being innocent, chose to accept a caution instead of undergo the humiliation of a trial as a paeodophile. To do so meant admitting guilt and being placed on the sex offenders register.

Operation Ore may turn out to be one of the worst miscarriages of justice ever seen in Britain. Chris Saltrese, a Merseyside solicitor, believes he can prove that scores of men caught up in Operation Ore were victims of identity theft. The Appeal Court has yet to rule on the single test case brought by Saltrese. But whatever the eventual outcome, it will be too late for some. In addition to the hundreds of innocent men who lost their jobs and families as a result of police heavy-handedness, stupidity or wilfulness, at least 39 of the accused have already committed suicide. Many were guilty of nothing more than having their credit card stolen and used to subscribe to a website that they would never have dreamt of visiting.

No apology needed

ALTHOUGH POLITICIANS seem increasingly reluctant to apologise for ever cocking anything up themselves, in recent years they have developed an extraordinary penchant for saying 'sorry' for historical events that had absolutely nothing to do with them.

- In August 2007, London mayor Ken Livingstone tearfully apologised for London's role in the slave trade, which had ended 200 years earlier.

- The year before, Prime Minister Tony Blair expressed deep sorrow over Britain's role in the slave trade while, in 1997, he apologised for the Irish potato famine (ended 1852).

- In 2008, Canadian Prime Minister Stephen Harper apologised for the way native Canadians had been treated.

- Australian Prime Minister Kevin Rudd apologised to the country's Aborigines in 2008 for government policies that 'inflicted profound grief, suffering and loss on these our fellow Australians'. Some Aboriginal leaders called it a 'cut-price sorry', with one pointing out that 'blackfellas will get the words, the whitefellas keep the money'.

- In 2000, Pope John Paul II went into a millennium apology overdrive, saying 'sorry' for all the sins of Catholics over the centuries, including those committed against Jews, women and minorities.

- Pope John Paul II apologised again in 2004, this time for the annihilation of Constantinople by Christian Crusaders eight hundred years earlier, in 1204.

If politicians wearing hair shirts were proving popular with the public, Gordon Brown didn't want to be left out. So he made an apology in September 2009. Did he apologise for selling half Britain's gold reserves a decade earlier, driving down the price by announcing the sale in advance and losing a potential £9.1bn as gold climbed from $250 to over $1,000 an ounce? Did he

apologise for changing the tax treatment of dividends in 1997, which has lost pension funds over £100 billion and destroyed the pensions of millions of people? Did he apologise for the cock-up over the tax credits system that saw some of the poorest families in Britain having to pay back money wrongly paid out, while many others never saw money due to them? Did he apologise for Government debt reaching the highest level since the Second World War?

No, he apologised for the way Alan Turing, the mathematician and codebreaker whose extraordinary skills helped to shorten the war, was treated when he broke the laws against homosexuality in the 1950s.

Brown's apology was a direct response to one of the most popular Downing Street online petitions at the time, with over 30,000 signatures. Another successful petition (over 40,000 signatures) brought a promise to abandon the 08 premium rate telephone number NHS patients had to ring.

But there has still been no response to the No. 1 petition to the Prime Minister at the time, with over 70,000 signatures – the one that consisted of the single word 'resign'.

performance time

When a theatre tells you that a play starts at 7.30, you expect it to start at 7.30. When a concert is supposed to start at 8, that's the time you reckon it should begin. But when a cinema tells you that the 'programme time' is 8.40, you can be certain that the film won't start until 9.00.

These days, most cinemas don't even use the phrase 'performance time'; they simply state the name of the film and give the time as 8.40.

And so, no matter how many years of cinemagoing you've got under your belt, you find yourself there 20 minutes early – and it always is twenty minutes – having to sit through awful adverts for products you would never dream of buying and trailers for films you'd never dream of seeing. If you go to the movies regularly, they will be the same trailers and ads you saw last time. You know it's going to happen, but you can't resist the voice inside your head saying, 'What if this is the one time in the history of cinema when a film actually starts at the advertised time?'

In the really old days, of course, cinemas did have programmes. As well as the main film, adverts and trailers you'd get a short and maybe even a B-movie. Now, they just want to make sure you have enough time to stock up on popcorn and overpriced fizzy syrup. That'll still give you 15 minutes to fume in the dark while you wait for the film to begin, and calculate just how many hours of your life have been spent in the same way.

Double number you first thought of

WE'RE ALL USED to workmen's estimates that appear, when we come to pay the bill, to have been little more than a guess. But when it comes to spending taxpayers' money, you'd like to think that ministers and civil servants would be more careful than to spout the number they first think of. Not a bit of it; and they seem to have no idea what to do when projects begin spiralling out of control. But why worry? It's not their money after all.

In 2007, the Taxpayers' Alliance examined 300 Government projects, including roads, hospitals, IT systems and science facilities which had either been finished since the start of 2005 or were still ongoing. They found that, in aggregate, they were £23 billion above the original estimates, which is about £900 for every household in the UK, the average overrun being 33.7%. 57% of projects overran, with only 14% coming in under budget.

The Alliance found a catalogue of deception in the way that departments tried to conceal budget overruns. The MoD often cut the units ordered, so that instead of 48,000 Bowman radios, they bought 43,000 and, hey presto, the cost was below the original estimate. However, when they cut an order for Nimrod spy planes, they still ended up paying £3.5 billion for 12, instead of the original £2.8 billion for 21.

In the case of the gargantuan NHS IT project to link patients' records (NPfIT), the Public Accounts Committee found that those in charge of the project were blissfully unaware how much was being spent. Richard Bacon MP asked how much had been committed irrevocably to the project. Richard Granger, head of Connecting for Health, replied: 'I do not have that exact figure right now.' 'You do not know?' thundered Bacon. 'You do not know? We have been told that this programme is going to cost £2.3 billion, we have been told it is going to cost £6.2 billion, we have been told it is going to cost £6.8 billion and we have been told it is going to cost £12.4 billion or £12.6 billion. Lord Warner, the Minister, said only three weeks ago on 30 May that it was going to cost £20 billion and you still cannot tell this Committee how much has been committed to it?'

Reassuring, isn't it, that our money is in such safe hands. Here are a few projects, past and current, where the initial estimate seems to have been worked out on the back of an envelope:

- The 2012 Olympics: original estimate £2.4 billion. The current estimate is £9.3 billion, and is expected to rise further.
- NPfIT: original estimate £2.3 billion, current estimate £20 billion and rising.
- Total other current public IT projects: £1.6 billion over budget and total of 86 years late.
- Benefits Payment Card project: abandoned January 2000, £1 billion over budget at time.
- Tax credits system: Software completely up the swanee. Estimated overspend £2 billion.
- Fire Service FIREeControl IT system: estimate £120 million. Current estimate £190 million and minimum of 2 years late.
- The Millennium Dome: original estimate £399 million, eventual cost 'estimated' to be over £1 billion.
- Parliamentary building Portcullis House: estimate £148 million, final cost £233 million.
- Top 20 MoD procurement projects: original estimate £24.4 billion. Revised estimate £27 billion, total of 36 years late.

- Holyrood, Scottish Parliament: estimate £40 million, final cost £414 million (average cost of office space in Edinburgh, £1,544 per square metre; Holyrood, £6,686).

- Astute class submarine: original budget, £2.6 billion. Revised budget, £3.6 billion and 41 months late.

- Type 45 destroyer: original estimate £5 billion. Revised budget, £6.1 billion.

Of course, large-scale public overruns are nothing new. Here are a few choice examples from the archives:

- The Jubilee Line: original estimate £2.1 billion. Final cost £3.5 billion.

- The Channel Tunnel: original estimate £4.8 billion. Final Cost, £10 billion.

- British Library: £450m over budget and 15 years late.

- Humber Bridge: estimate £28 million. By time bridge opened, had cost £151 million.

- The Barbican: original estimate £8 million, final cost £187 million.

- Concorde: original estimate £45 million, final cost £1.01 billion.

- The Suez Canal: opened in 1869 at 20 times its original estimate.

- Sydney Opera House: famous not just because of its distinctive shape, but also because it cost, at A$102 million, 15 times its original estimate. At least that one isn't Whitehall's fault.

awesome

The word originally meant 'inspiring awe', and was not a word to be used lightly. 'There was something awesome in the thought of the solitary mortal standing by the open window and summoning in from the gloom outside the spirits of the nether world,' said Sir Arthur Conan Doyle; 'The Soviet Union has conducted the greatest military buildup in the history of man, building arsenals of awesome offensive weapons,' pronounced Ronald Reagan at his second inaugural address in 1985.

The word then came to mean 'exceptional', and is now so commonplace that it simply means 'of interest'. When we hear Daniel Radcliffe pronounce: 'Some people think I'm gay when I meet them, which I think is awesome', we know the word has lost all meaning.

terms and conditions apply

Although you'll occasionally see this phrase in print, you're more likely to heard it spoken at high speed at the end of advertisements for mortgages, loans and other commercial services.

It's the verbal equivalent of the asterisk, and is there to signify that there's an awful lot the advertisers aren't telling you about how restrictive the service they're offering really is. In other words: what we've just said sounds like a fantastic offer, but that's because it probably isn't true.

Up to 100% or more

WE WERE TAUGHT at school that 0% is nothing, and 100% of something is everything. It was a neatly defined mathematical universe, precisely bordered by certainties. But now that inflation has hit percentages, we can no longer be so certain . . .

- Tony Blair, on various occasions, asserted '101% support' for Brown's proposal to lower income tax to 10p in 1995, for the Israeli Prime Minister in 1999, the Olympic bid in 2004, and for a police raid in 2006.
- Freddie Flintoff raised the game by offering to give '110% for England' in the Cricket World Cup.
- South African cricket captain Shaun Pollock insisted his team would be able to clear their name after a scandal 'by giving 120%'.
- As Conservative leader, William Hague expressed '150% confidence' in Ann Widdecombe's abilities as shadow Home Secretary.
- All this pussyfooting around was blown away by Sven-Goran Eriksson's assertion that Wayne Rooney was '300% confident' that he would play in the 2006 World Cup.

But this is all just rhetoric, of course. So what are we to make of the claim on packets of Peperami that they contain 'Pork (150%)'. Come again? Well, Unilever – the manufacturers – do qualify this by explaining: 'Made with 37.5g pork per 25g finished product, as some moisture is lost during curing and drying'.

OK, let's do the maths. 37.5g per 25g pork is, rather neatly, 150%. So if Peperami is made from '150%' pork, that means the finished product contains 100% pork after curing and drying. Which leaves no room whatsoever for the delicious salt, glucose, spices, monosodium glutamate, sodium 5 ribonucleotides, garlic powder and sodium nitrite that are also listed as ingredients.

Perhaps they're just giving 110%.

Green grow the turbines

IN OUR EFFORTS to be 'green' and environmentally friendly, we encounter a plethora of words and phrases, the meaning and definition of which is infuriatingly unclear.

In June 2009, *The Guardian* reported a study presented to Congress which found over 98% of supposedly natural and environmentally friendly products on US supermarket shelves made false or misleading boasts, known as 'greenwashing'. In the UK, the ASA say they've seen a growing number of 'greenwashing' complaints, with oil companies, car makers and airlines among the worst offenders. Chairman Lord Smith of Finsbury said they found 'claims about being carbon neutral, zero carbon emissions and use of words like "sustainable", "organic", "100 per cent recycled" or "greenest car in its class". We have come across quite a number where claims are exaggerated or misleading or, in some cases, severely exaggerated.'

Friends of the Earth complained about a Shell ad showing an oil refinery with flowers coming out of its chimneys, saying 'we use our waste CO_2 to grow flowers'. As the proportion used was just 0.325% of its CO_2 output, the ASA smacked Shell's wrists.

In this area, not everything is as green as it sounds . . .

Green cars

There's no official definition of 'green', which allows Gordon Brown to announce, as a green initiative, that he wants Britain to be a world leader in producing and using electric cars. They may produce no fumes and *look* green, but are powered by electricity, 75% of which is currently generated by fossil fuels.

As for more conventional cars, the International Automobile Federation Foundation's EcoTest found in 2008 that some new 'environmentally friendly' models were worse polluters than they had been five years earlier. Cars from Renault, Honda and Daihatsu were the worst offenders, with the Renault

Scenic, boasting it was 'the UK's greenest car', scoring 61% for 'greenness' against 66% in the previous test. The FIA Foundation said car buyers were 'lost in a green vehicles fog . . . Motorists need independent, accurate and up-to-date information.'

Freedom Food

This assurance mark from the RSPCA was set up 'to improve the welfare of farm animals and offer consumers a higher welfare choice'. But the Freedom Food label can apply to hens and chickens that spend their entire lives indoors. Some freedom!

● *Don't throw away . . .*
0.325% of Shell's CO_2 output.

Even worse, in February 2009, Channel Five found several Freedom Food farms where birds were kept under appalling

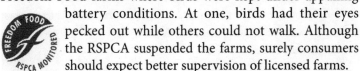

battery conditions. At one, birds had their eyes pecked out while others could not walk. Although the RSPCA suspended the farms, surely consumers should expect better supervision of licensed farms.

The Freedom Food label also covers farmed fish. In 2008, Freedom Food producer Marine Harvest admitted shooting seals to protect its farmed salmon. The RSPCA said, 'Under the RSPCA's standards, this is very much a last resort and the lethal method used must be humane.' But why is the RSPCA involved at all in a scheme that results in seals being killed?

Fairtrade

Fair to whom? The idea of ensuring that more money goes to Third World farmers rather than multinationals is admirable. But the *Economist* lamented that 'certification is predicated on political assumptions about the best way to organise labour'. Fairtrade prefers cooperatives to individual farmers, even though this often leads to corruption.

In January 2009, *The Times* reported that Fairtrade tea plantation workers had seen no improvement in their lives. Others have pointed out that Fairtrade, an organisation which has grown to become a global enterprise overseeing $4 billion of sales in 2008, does nothing to encourage mechanisation or technology, condemning people to an agrarian subsistence.

Fairtrade's success also squeezes out other ethical organisations, such as Ugandan outfit Good African Coffee (slogan: 'Trade not Aid') and Café Britt, whose UK distributor went out of business. Most Fairtrade coffee is brought to Europe to be roasted and packaged by – surprise, surprise – the big multinationals, even though unroasted beans deteriorate. Café Britt's farmers do everything themselves and so receive far more of the price.

With supermarkets pocketing around a third of the inflated Fairtrade price, Nick Gading of retail analysts Verdict says: 'People would be shocked to find out how little really goes back to the producers.' That's if they can find out. Although £700m was spend on Fairtrade products in the UK in 2008, the Fairtrade Foundation's Annual Review for 2008/9 astoundingly contains not one concrete figure on what producers receive.

Biofuel

Biofool, more like. The EU insists that we use more biofuel, even though just one tank of biofuel could feed an African for a year and the move to biofuel crops is accelerating deforestation at an alarming rate. In 2008, as crop prices soared and parts of the world saw food riots, United Nations food expert Jean Ziegler called biofuel production, using crops that should feed people to burn in cars instead, 'a crime against humanity'.

Barbara Helfferich, on behalf of the EU Environment Commission, said: 'There is no question for now of suspending the target fixed for biofuels. You can't change a political objective without risking a debate on all the other objectives.'

So biofuels must still make up 10% of the EU's 27 states automobile fuel by 2020. It does not matter that, as Ziegler, says 'children are dying' as a result. It does not matter that Peter Brabeck-Letmathe, head of Nestlé, the world's largest food company, says that 'to grant enormous subsidies for biofuel production is morally unacceptable and irresponsible. There will be nothing left to eat'.

It does not matter that massive deforestation to grow biofuel crops will pour CO_2 into the atmosphere, reduce our supply of oxygen and accelerate global warming. Yet it is to avoid *exactly that* that the EU is forcing growing biofuel production. But then, as Zielger also claimed, EU subsidies for surplus agricultural products exported to Africa 'completely ruins African agriculture'. Common sense seems in short supply.

Recycling

We all know how important it is to recycle. Well, perhaps not all of us. Some of those trendy Swedes, who first introduced so many environmental ideas, think it's crazy and deluded. They include the former director-general of Sweden's environmental protection agency, the former campaign manager of Keep Sweden Tidy, and the former MDs of three waste-collection companies. They argue that burning rubbish is actually better for the environment than recycling, and that technological improvements mean incineration is cleaner and could generate electricity, reducing dependence on fossil fuels.

Local authorities in the UK have been ordered to recycle 30% of waste by 2010. A spokesman for DEFRA said incineration 'causes dangerous emissions, raises public concern and sends out a negative message about re-use'. So yet again, instead of engaging in discussion about what might be best for the environment, we are simply told to toe the line and ignore advice from some of those with the greatest expertise in the area.

Greenland

Imagine you're Eric the Red, fleeing Iceland in exile in around 1000AD. You've discovered this huge new country, and you want to attract migrants to come and live in it with you. What do you call it?

The name 'Greenland' is a marketing exercise, a name specifically created to entice visitors. It's certainly a hell of a lot more appealing than 'Iceland'.

no offence

This innocuous little phrase has allowed more insults and *faux pas* to slip by unchallenged than just about any other: 'No offence, but you look really fat in that skirt.'

What the phrase really means is: 'I'm about to say something really offensive, but because I've told you in advance you can't claim to be offended, we've already agreed that I'm just telling it like it is, so if you get offended you're just over-reacting.'

with the greatest respect

See *no offence*.

'What you as the City of London have done for financial services, we as a Government intend to do for the economy as a whole.'

Gordon Brown, Chancellor, Mansion House speech
26 June 2002

Are you my baby's father?

'HI. MY NAME IS KAREN and I am from Denmark, and this here is my baby boy.'

So begins the heart-rending YouTube video featuring a pretty blonde girl and her young child, who goes on to explain how she met a tourist in Copenhagen and, in the spirit of typical Danish hospitality, had sex with him and later bore his child.

'I'm doing this because I'm trying to find August's father,' she goes on to explain. 'I don't remember where you're from ... I don't even remember your name.'

The video, which has had hundreds of thousands of YouTube viewings, links to a website featuring images of Karen and her baby, commenting: 'I'm really overwhelmed and touched by all your nice comments and support from all over the world.'

The problem is that the baby's name isn't August, and he isn't Karen's. Karen doesn't have any children. And her name isn't Karen, she's an actress named Ditte Arnth Jørgensen.

The whole idea was dreamt up by VisitDenmark as a bizarre publicity stunt. VisitDenmark CEO Dorte Kiilerich initially defended the story, saying it was intended to create a positive view of Denmark: 'Karen's story shows that Denmark is a broad-minded country where you can do what you want. The film is a good example of independent, dignified, Danish women who dare to make their own choices.'

Although Kiilerich later apologised for having 'offended a lot of people', the Grey ad agency, who made the film, still hailed it as 'the most successful viral advert ever'. So at least someone was a winner out of all this.

Claiming it's the truth

AS THE RECESSION BIT, Britain's insurers reported a steep rise in the number of fraudulent claims to £1.7 billion. Admiral and Aviva both reckoned that suspicious claims jumped by around a third between 2008 and 2009, with inflated car repair bills, fictitious injuries and imaginary goods being stolen among the scams being tried. The Association of British Insurers reckons that, as a result this and more organised criminal activity, we all pay an extra £44 a year in premiums. In 2008, 3.6 million Britons said they didn't think it was wrong to submit a fraudulent insurance claim. In 2009, the figure jumped to 4.7 million.

However, the insurance companies, also feeling the pinch, have been on the case. They have rejected more claims than ever before and some even use voice stress analysers, which they believe give an indication that the person on the phone might be lying, even though most people probably find it incredibly stressful dealing with insurance companies in any circumstances.

Lloyds TSB reported some of the weirdest insurance claims they'd received:

- A digital radio was ruined when the policyholder's granddaughter put it in a pond to 'play music to the fish to make them dance'.
- A disposable barbecue tray melted a hole in an asphalt roof, the coals dropping into the room below.
- Home owners returned home to find their carpet covered in white paint after their labrador managed to dip his tail in a tray of white emulsion.

- A man refurbishing his gun accidentally shot his TV.
- A magpie flew into a room, picked up a policyholder's spectacles, and flew off with them.

- A collection of sex appliances was stolen. The claim was accompanied by a set of receipts.
- One customer reported a broken bed and bedpost, saying 'nothing gets in the way of passion'.

Other insurance companies have reported a similar rash of mystifying and unlikely claims, including:

- A claim for hospital bills after a British man in Athens was admiring a group of women in bikinis and walked into a bus shelter, breaking his nose.
- A motorist somehow filled her tank with shampoo from a bottle rather than petrol.
- A pensioner who was sick over the side of a cruise ship lost his false teeth and claimed for new dentures under 'lost baggage'.
- 'A deer headbutted the windscreen of my car, after being enticed by the yellow tax disc'.
- A motorist claimed that a camel had kicked and damaged his car at a garden centre, and provided CCTV footage to back it up.
- Another car was damaged by a naked pedestrian jumping up and down on the roof.
- A family had their camping holiday ruined when an Army parachutist landed on their tent. The insurance company didn't pay up.
- A man furious with a speed camera that had snapped him, tried to break it by ramming the post. He succeeded only in smashing up his car and then claimed for it, insisting it was an accident.

Your train is delayed

JUST HOW HONEST are the explanations we hear so regularly about why trains are late? Blogger Dave Cross noticed that while BBC News claimed that his section of the Northern Line was suspended due to 'overrunning engineering work', the SMS tube alert service from London Underground was rather more truthful: 'SEVERE DELAYS: Nrthrn from 7:16 – an earlier track search for a missing member of staff.'

Here are some more announcements heard by underground passengers, most of which are more honest than usual.

'I apologise for the delay but the computer controlling the signalling at Aldgate and Whitechapel has the Monday morning blues.'

'We apologise for the delays to services tonight, this is caused by extended intervals between trains.'

'Hello this is David speaking. I am the captain of your train, and we will be departing shortly. We will be cruising at an altitude of approximately zero feet and our scheduled arrival time in Morden is 3:15pm. The temperature in Morden is approximately 15 degrees celsius, and Morden is in the same time zone as Mill Hill East, so there's no need to adjust your watches.'

'I apologise for the delays to your service this evening. This is due to… Well, it's just a crap service isn't it?'

'This is the Line Control Room at Baker Street. The Bakerloo Line is running normally today, so you may expect delays to all destinations.'

'Ladies and gentlemen, I'm sorry for the delay, I have just been informed this is due to people on the roof of the train ahead. Yes, you are probably thinking some of the things I am, but that's what I've been told by my control.'

'Apparently, this train is no longer terminating at Barking, but is in fact, terminating here. I'm sorry about this but I too was under the impression that this train was going to Barking, but they have other ideas. I mean, why tell me – I'm merely the driver.'

'Your delay this evening is caused by the line controller suffering from elbow and backside syndrome, not knowing one from the other. I'll let you know any further information as soon as I'm given any.'

'Ladies and gentlemen we will shortly be arriving at Waterloo, then I think we will carry right on through the Channel Tunnel and spend the weekend in Paris'.

'Beggars are operating on this train. Please do not encourage these professional beggars. If you have any spare change, please give it to a registered charity. Failing that, give it to me.'

'I apologise for the delay leaving the station, ladies and gentlemen. This is due to a crustie masturbating on the train at Edgware Road. Someone has activated the alarm and he is being removed from the train.'

'May I remind all passengers that there is strictly no smoking allowed on any part of the Underground. However, if you are smoking a joint it is only fair that you pass it round the rest of the carriage'.

'We are now travelling through Baker Street, as you can see Baker Street is closed. It would have been nice if they had actually told me, so I could tell you, but no, they don't think about things like that.'

'Welcome aboard the Flintstones railway, once I get my feet on the floor and start running we should be on our way'.

'Ladies and gentlemen, upon departing the train may I remind you to take your rubbish with you. Despite the fact that you are in something that is metal, fairly round, filthy and smells, this is a tube train and not a bin on wheels.'

And a few announcements from the railways:

'On behalf of Virgin Trains I'd like to apologise that you had to put up with such an awful journey, and can only hope that your day doesn't get any worse.' *Virgin service from London to Manchester*

'We apologise for the late departure from Norwich, which was a result of the driver having had his car wheel-clamped.' *Central Trains from Norwich to Liverpool*

'Some charlie's used an alarm handle as a coat hook.'
Thameslink, London to Bedford

'This train is delayed as the guard has been taken away by the police. We hope to find you another one in half an hour.'

'We wish to apologise most sincerely to the passengers who have recently arrived on the Royal Highlander from Inverness. Your train was delayed for several hours due to a locomotive failure near Drumochter. Then the overhead wires came down near Wigan, so your train was diverted via Manchester. A passenger was taken ill, causing the train to have to wait for an ambulance to arrive at Stockport. Finally, you were diverted via Northampton, due to signalling equipment failure south of Rugby.'

Your call is important to us

IS THERE ANY PHRASE which causes the blood pressure to spike more than 'customer service'? How are we served by being forced to use a premium rate phone number to contact a company to complain about their product? How are we served by being made to play a game of telephone keypad sudoku in order to win ourselves a place in an indeterminate queue, while being played tinny music we loathe? And if we aren't cut off after half an hour's wait, while being constantly told that 'your call is important to us', how are we served by talking to somebody we can barely understand in a faraway country?

An ICM survey found that callers wasted an average of five minutes before speaking to a real person, if they got through to one at all. A third of calls don't even result in talking to a human being. In total, we waste 60 million hours a year holding on customer service lines, paying over £300 million on premium rate phone calls, sometimes to ring up the phone companies themselves.

It's often just as bad when you deal with companies face to face. We'd write in and complain, if we didn't know that they'd treat our letter with as much disdain as our phone call.

With a few honourable exceptions, it's as if the heads of every company in the land got together and decided that, far from the customer always being right, they are a nuisance and should just sod off.

- Try querying your energy or phone bill. Citizens Advice say that these are the worst companies, with over four in five customers unhappy about the level of service.

- Try changing a train or plane booking. The cost is usually prohibitive. Get on the wrong train by mistake and you may be charged the maximum possible fare.

- Withdraw your own money from a 'convenient' ATM and you may have to pay £1.75 for the privilege.

- Agree to a 10 per cent discount card at Dorothy Perkins, only to discover it's a high interest rate credit card.
- Be asked to pay 12.5% service charge in a restaurant, and still be encouraged to leave a tip.
- Find cards pushed through your front door to say 'we called when you were out', when a simple push on the doorbell would have told them that you weren't.
- Fume at companies that won't put phone numbers on correspondence or their website.
- Being rung by your bank by someone who won't tell you what it's about unless you divulge your security details.

What is utterly infuriating about their behaviour is that it is appalling business practice. Every company in the land must surely know one of the most basic business maxims: it is much cheaper to keep a customer than to win a new one.

We suggest that before you ring any large organisation, you consult one of our favourite websites, *www.saynoto0870.com*. This admirable resource provides real phone numbers for many companies that don't cost extra to ring, or which can be called out of your phone package's inclusive minutes.

You may not get through any more quickly, but you may feel a little happier at knowing that you've deprived them of just a little of the profit they crave at the expense of that phrase so rarely heard these days, 'customer satisfaction'.

Health and safety

WE'RE USED TO READING ludicrous stories of 'health and safety madness' in the press. Stories of how schoolchildren must now wear goggles when using BluTak, of 40 benches having to be removed from a crematorium for being three inches too low, of Health and Safety executives themselves having to give 48 hours notice and wait for a porter before moving an office chair.

Sometimes, though, we come across a health and safety story that's not just daft, it's downright dangerous. Such is the case of 'safety' socket covers, of which millions have been sold in the UK to anxious parents.

For a start, they're not needed. Since 1949, all electrical sockets in the UK contain an internal barrier that lifts when the top pin of a plug is inserted. When the plug is removed, the lower holes – which carry the current – are completely shielded. In order to gain access to them, a child would first have to press a suitably-sized object, such as a screwdriver, hard into the top hole.

You can't take a standard plug, turn it upside down and stick it into the hole to lift the shutter, because the wall gets in the way and the plug isn't flexible. A child could, however, take a 'safety cover' and press it into the hole upside-down, because they're made of flimsy plastic which can be bent into place.

Tight regulations control the design of both sockets and electrical plugs. But there are no regulations covering 'safety plugs', with the result that some are so poorly made that they pop out of the socket, allowing safety pins and paperclips to be easily inserted into the open holes beneath. Among those singled out in a European Commission report were those sold by Mothercare and IKEA, as being notably prone to popping out. Health and safety, indeed.

● *An inverted safety plug opens live sockets*

Is organic food worth it?

MANY OF US LIKE to eat healthily. In the UK, we spend over £1.5 billion each year on organic food. But what exactly does 'organic' mean? There are EU regulations for organic food. Growers, processors and importers must be certified. The Soil Association has set its own standards for areas not covered, like fish farming, textiles and beauty care and health products.

We admit that we often buy organic food ourselves but, as with 'green' and 'carbon neutral', things aren't clear cut when it comes to matters 'organic'.

Omega-3 fish oils are said to be incredibly good for us. Research demonstrating that organic milk has more omega-3 than conventional milk compared the milk of an organic herd, reared outdoors in lush pastures, with a dairy herd kept indoors and fed dry food. Hardly a like-for-like comparison.

The Swedish University of Agricultural Scientists found that, contrary to earlier studies, organic milk did not contain significantly higher levels of vitamins A and E, while other studies show that organic milk is actually less healthy than conventional milk. UHT milk is apparently even less healthy, yet 80% of the world's organic milk is UHT and, because it's more environmentally-friendly (it doesn't have to be moved as quickly or refrigerated), governments are encouraging a shift to UHT.

Less taste, less nutritious

Food scientists at Strathclyde University found that organic chicken breasts contained fewer omega-3 fatty acids and lower levels of antioxidants than regular supermarket breasts. Not only did some organic breasts have double the cholesterol but, despite costing up to twice as much, they didn't taste as good.

Alistair Paterson, who co-authored the study, said, 'You are not getting any nutritional benefit from buying organic chicken. You could be better off buying conventional or free-range chicken.'

He added that synthetic vitamin supplements in conventional feed would result in a better taste, but were prohibited by organic farming rules.

In July 2009, the Food Standards Agency found that organic food in general had no nutritional benefit in vitamins or minerals over cheaper, conventional food. Dr Alan Dangour, of the London school of Hygiene and Tropical Medicine, said: 'Our review indicates that there is currently no evidence to support the selection of organically over conventionally produced foods on the basis of nutritional superiority.' The extensive study was challenged by organic farmers, who said it did not take into account the effect of chemicals used in conventional farming or organic farming's environmental benefits.

Biochemist Anthony Trewavas of Edinburgh University found that organic food uses more energy per tonne of food because its yields are lower. In addition, it requires double the land, leaving less scope for un-farmed land to increase biodiversity. A study for DEFRA found that organic tomatoes required 1.9 times the energy and organic chickens 25% more, while organic milk created 20% more CO_2.

We are often told that eating healthy organic food stops us taking in huge amounts of cancer-causing pesticides. Sir John Krebs of the Food Standards Agency, however, pointed out in *Nature* magazine that 'A single cup of coffee contains natural carcinogens equal to at least a year's worth of carcinogenic synthetic residues in the diet.'

Air freight: the hidden cost

34% of our organic food was imported into the UK in 2005, mostly by air. Baby corn can travel 5,900 miles from Thailand, while blueberries are flown here in the winter from New Zealand. The Soil Association proposed banning the label 'organic' from anything flown to the UK.

Some, such as the Co-op, opposed the move: not only would it worsen third world poverty, harming subsistence farmers, but they may be using more environmentally-friendly farming methods. The objectors pointed out that some air-freighted food results in lower carbon emissions than domestically-grown food on mechanised farms.

Are tomatoes grown outdoors in Spain worse than those grown in centrally-heated greenhouses here, which give off 100 times the CO_2? It's complicated. As Gareth Thomas, Minister for Trade and Development, said: 'Driving 6.5 miles to buy your shopping emits more carbon than flying a pack of Kenyan green beans to the UK.' The Soil Association has backtracked and is currently monitoring the situation.

There are growing numbers of organic beauty products but EU regulations don't cover these, although the Soil Association has set its own standards. There have been an alarming number of instances of food fraud, with poorly-produced meat, eggs and fish labelled as organic, raking in millions of pounds for fraudsters.

Organic products are more expensive, but the arguments in their favour are by no means as clear-cut as is often claimed. In too many instances, the use of the word 'organic', particularly on items not covered by regulations, is little more than an excuse for grabbing a much higher profit margin.

Having said all that, we still often buy organic and insist on free-range eggs. Then a study by the Scottish Agricultural College found that free-range and barn-reared hens had almost double the number of bone fractures as battery hens, mostly from crashing into other birds as they try to fly in what is still a restricted space. We considered keeping our own hens, but the free-range foxes would no doubt get them first.

All-natural ingredients

IF A FOOD product makes this sweeping claim, then it must by law include only ingredients that are naturally sourced, rather than those produced by combining chemicals. If you've a vegetarian, though, you need to look closely at these 'natural' colourings and flavourings: many additives turn out to be animal-based.

The red food dye cochineal, also known as carmine, is produced from an insect – *Dactylopius coccus* – which lives mainly in South America. It eats red cactus berries, whose pigment is stored in their bodies. It takes over 150,000 killed, dried and crushed insects to make each kilogram of food dye. You'll find dead insect dye in pink grapefruit juice, strawberry yoghurts and many other products.

In 2007, Mars dropped plans to include rennet (extracted from the stomachs of dead calves) in Mars bars, Snickers, Maltesers and Galaxy, following an outcry from vegetarians. But they still use it in Twix, Milky Way and Celebrations. A spokesman for Mars UK explained it away: 'At no stage have we claimed that they are suitable for vegetarians or that they would be.'

In fact, our foods and other household products are full of animal-derived ingredients. Here are just a few of the many examples uncovered by the Vegetarian and Vegan Foundation:

- Casein, a protein made from milk, is found in most condoms
- Chitin, used in shampoos and moisturisers, is made from insects and crustacea
- Collagen, the source of gelatine, is made from boiled animal connective tissue
- Down, used in bedding, is usually derived from slaughtered ducks and geese. Eastern European goose down is frequently plucked from live birds
- Glycerine, used in toothpaste, is often made from animal fat

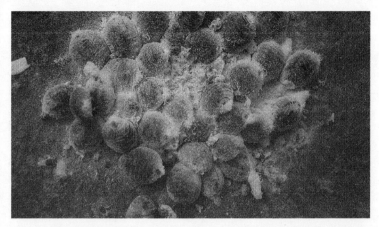

- *Female cochineal insects before going into strawberry milkshake*

- Hormone Replacement Therapy (HRT) is sometimes made from the urine of pregnant mares
- Insulin, a treatment for diabetes, comes from the pancreas of sheep or pigs
- Isinglass, used to clarify alcoholic drinks, is made from the swim bladders of sturgeon
- Keratin, a protein used in shampoo and conditioners, is made from hair, horns, hooves and feathers
- Lecithin, used largely in confectionery, is a fatty material mainly found in nerve tissues and blood
- Pepsin, used to make cheese, is an enzyme taken from the gastric juices of farm animals
- Stearic acid, used in medicine and toiletries, is made from animal fat
- Tallow, used in soap and candles, comes from hard fat around the kidneys of slaughtered cattle.

index

● *Elvis in concert. In 2010. He looks pretty good for a 75-year-old who's been dead for 32 years.*